Celebrating

the

Celtic Saints

For My Wife

Beverley

Celebrating the Celtic Saints

as candles

on a stand

toby d. griffen

Templegate Publishers
Springfield, Illinois

Text, music and illustrations
copyright © 1998 by Toby D. Griffen
First published in the United States by
Templegate Publishers
302 E. Adams St.
P.O. Box 5152
Springfield, Illinois 62705-5152

ISBN 0-87243-237-8

Library of Congress Catalog Card
Number 98-60110

Toby D. Griffen is the composer of both
the words and music of the hymns which
appear in the text.

pReface

the age of saints

For Western Christendom, the Dark Ages correspond to the three days in the tomb of our Lord Jesus Christ. Just as Jesus died on the cross on Good Friday, so the Western Church lay shattered by the pagan barbarians who trampled over the remains of the Roman Empire.

During the period in the tomb, there was no assurance for the Disciples that Jesus would indeed arise from the grave. Saint Peter denied him, and the other Apostles scattered and huddled in their rooms, fearing for their very lives. In the period of the Dark Ages, the Western Church lay just as helpless, fearing for its life as well.

Just as Christ arose from the tomb on Easter Morning, however, so the Western Church arose from the ashes of the fall, helped up by the descendants of the barbarians who had brought it down. Thus, the parallel would appear to be complete in the familiar pattern of death and Resurrection.

But there is another, more profound analogy between the Dark Ages and the tomb. When Christ arose from the dead to conquer Death, he passed on to his Disciples the great Sustainer of the Trinity - the Holy Spirit. This Spirit had sustained him in death, as it has sustained all Christians ever since.

The sustaining spirit of the Dark Ages was the loosely confederated, deeply spiritual Celtic Church of Britain and Ireland. In the face of the Germanic invasions, the British Church held firm in the

British Isles and in Brittany and became a wall between the pagans and the Irish Church. The Irish Church was thus able to record the precious teachings of Christendom and then to join together with the beleaguered Britons to spread the Light once again throughout all of Europe.

This was the Age of Saints - the saints who long ago held firm to the Holy Spirit and passed it on to us.

the celebrations

This book presents eighteen of the most prominent (and more or less historically identifiable) saints from the Celtic Church of the Dark Ages along with celebrations of the Celtic Cross and of All Celtic Saints. These were not angels sent by God to deliver us, but human beings – just like us – who rose to the challenge and preserved the church. So when we celebrate the lives of these people of God, we do not worship them or pray to them; but rather, we look to them as models of strength and wisdom to guide us in our lives as people of God.

This book can, of course, be read alone in silence and thoughtful meditation. But as Christ is present when two or three are gathered in his Name, so ought we truly to celebrate in groups of believers. These celebrations are particularly suited to such community gatherings and incorporate not only a commemoration of the saints, but also liturgies (or services) of the Word and of prayer.

To help guide group services, the order of celebrations for the saints themselves follow the feast days through the year, with at least one celebration per month. The celebration of the Celtic Cross is presented first, however, as this sets the themes that recur throughout the year; and the celebration of All Celtic Saints is last, as this provides both a closure and a beginning.

Each celebration begins with the name of the saint and the Christian quality being celebrated in his or her memory. In between the name and the quality is a symbol by which to remember and meditate on the saint.

The commemoration of the saint is precisely what the Latin roots of the word *commemorate* mean: We remember together the life of the saint. This is not a complete biography, but a reflection on the saint's life in view of the quality being celebrated. While some information for the summary of the saint's life is taken from the Lives (stories of the saints, usually written down much later),these fanciful stories overladen with miracles have been examined to see what the most noteworthy of the saint's virtues may have been.

We give the feast day (or days) for the saint, so that the celebration might be coordinated with church services at the appropriate time. The recognized feast day also provides a criterion for whether or not a saint is to be considered authentic enough to be included. While there are many lists of Celtic saints and much debate on their authenticity, only those whose feast days are recorded in David Hugh Farmer's *The Oxford Dictionary of Saints* (third edition, Oxford, 1992) are included here.

The final section of the commemoration is devoted to the symbol found at the beginning of the celebration. This provides a visual focus for meditation, and it is recommended that after reading the section, celebrants should take the words to heart and contemplate the symbol, and to consider what other aspects of the saint they can call to mind. In group celebrations, this provides a moment of silence before the liturgies.

The term *liturgy* comes from a Greek word for service – both in the sense of a church meeting and in the sense of broader acts of dedication. The liturgies are thus the foundations for worship (especially of a group) and also an act of dedication not only to the saint being celebrated, but also to one another as we dedicate our lives to the qualities the saints showed to the people of God. The liturgy of the Word consists of an appropriate reading from Holy Scripture and of a meditation. All of the scriptural readings are from the Revised Standard Version of the Bible.

The meditation is a commentary on the lesson, and it is given in contemporary language. While it is based upon the Scripture, it is written in a way that should be consistent with the life of the saint being celebrated. We might approach the meditation in a frame of mind that would ponder what the saint would have to say about the Scripture in the light of what he or she might see in the world today.

The liturgy of prayer is entirely in "traditional" language – language used by many churches for prayer including the *thou* form (for example, *thou givest*) and the archaic third person singular (for example, *he or she giveth*). This language is used here to give the liturgy more of a prayerful feeling, for in prayer feeling is every bit as important as thought for making the connection with a God who knows both our feelings and our thoughts most intimately.

As it is used in many churches, the collect is a prayer that summarizes the lessons. Accordingly, this prayer "collects" the commemoration of the saint and the liturgy of the Word. It is a petitionary prayer, asking God for the quality of the saint we celebrate; but as in all such prayers, it is mostly intended to give us pause to consider how we might incorporate that quality within our lives in a way that would be pleasing to God.

Without music, the hymn can be read as a verse prayer – and indeed all hymns are prayers. It is most highly recommended, however, that the celebration include the music. As the word appeals to the reason, so the music appeals to the soul. Thus, the thoughts of the verse drawn together with the feelings of the music can touch the spirit.

Finally, two little prayers mark the completion of the celebration: a prayer of thanksgiving and a prayer for Grace. We should ever be mindful that God has sent us these saints to help guide us in the Way. Therefore, we should thank the Lord for providing them as our guides. Moreover, we should not simply be thankful and then leave the celebration; for as these saints have been sent to guide us, so we are intended to follow them. As always, we pray for God's Grace to give us these qualities.

the selection of saints

In every book of saints, the author must select which saints to include and, sadly, which saints not to include. The selection of the saints included in this book was guided by a need for balance. Too many books that deal with the Celtic saints include predominantly (or exclusively) the saints from Ireland or from Wales or from some other country. In the eighteen celebrations of particular saints, I sought a achieve a balance between the Gaelic and the Brythonic (*i.e.* the Celtic British) and to include representatives from every Celtic country. Unfortunately, this means that many worthy saints (such as Saints Kevin, Kentigern, Columbanus, etc.) were not included.

Moreover, I sought to include as great a proportion as possible of the women saints. God has provided us with men and women saints to inspire us all, but the scribes have traditionally favored the former. Thus, of the eighteen individual saints, six are women. While this is a larger proportion than usual, it is still rather too small – a consequence of being limited by the need to include only those whose lives are historically most reliable (and we are, once again, at the mercy of the scribes).

On the names of the saints, a couple of comments may be in order. While the Welsh know Saint Dubricius as Dyfrig, he preceded both the nation of Wales and the Welsh language. His name is a combination of Brythonic and Latin, and it is presented in its original form here because he was indeed the Papa of a great many churches not only in Wales, but also in what is today England. As such, he was a British saint and retains here his British name.

As for Saint Hildutus, the Latin form is admittedly quite rare today. In the spirit of balance, however, we should recognize that he is dear to the hearts not only of the Welsh who call him Illtud or Illtyd, but also of the Bretons who call him Eltut. So as to slight neither of these Christian peoples, let us use the Latin name which he himself used, for the differences in the Welsh and the Breton merely reflect changes in those languages from the original Hildutus.

Toby D. Griffen

table of contents

Celebrations

Bibliography and Indices

Celebrations

The Celtic Cross

A Celebration

of Unity

september 14
---
commemoration of the celtic cross

the celtic cross

The Celtic cross, or wheel cross, is one of the most widely recognized patterns of this Christian symbol. It comes to us through at least three different paths, or interpretations of its development. First, the circle with rays coming out from the center through its sides, top, and bottom had been a widespread symbol for the sun. In the Celtic world, this sun symbol had often been represented as an actual wheel with numerous spokes, deriving from the old belief that the sun was drawn by a chariot with wheels (see below). This interpretation is adaptable to Christianity on the basis that Christ is the Light of the world. Moreover, with its longer bottom line, the Celtic cross is reminiscent of the Star of Bethlehem, with the light directing us to the birth of the Savior.

The second path is more traditionally Christian and can be traced in the development of the cross itself on monuments in Britain and elsewhere. One of the earliest Christian symbols (even before the cross) was the Chi-Rho – a combination of the first two Greek letters in the name *Christos*, resembling a P over an X and often placed within a circle (or wreath). Gradually, the X was turned to become a crossed vertical and horizontal line, with the vertical line merging with the vertical line of the P. The loop of the P eventually disappeared, leaving us with the simple cross within a circle. By extending the lines beyond the circle, we have the traditional Celtic cross.

In a more basically Celtic tradition, however, the cross is indeed a "wheel cross." The wheel was a symbol of the Indo-European

4

peoples who had come into the West with the domesticated horse and the chariot. So the wheel in its simplest symbolic representation of a circle (the rim) with internal vertical and horizontal lines (the spokes) came to be associated with the Europeans and especially with the Celtic peoples. The Christian cross then is a traditional wheel symbol with the arms extended to form the cross of Christ superimposed upon the circular wheel. This interpretation is highly symbolic of Christ's lordship over the Celtic people, but it also represents a combination of Christianity with traditional Celtic spirituality.

One thing that the interpretation of the Celtic cross as a wheel cross does give us that is most characteristic of the Celtic way is the idea of connectedness. As the Celtic knots that often adorn it show a connectedness through the single unbroken thread, the wheel cross provides us with another unbroken symbol in a circle – often used as a symbol itself for the unity of the people of God – connected and embraced by the arms of the cross.

the symbol

Around the wheel of humanity, a never-ending knot binds all the people together. The significance of this knot is profound: We are all bound in a continuous thread. If any harm comes to any point on this thread, the very thing that binds us together is injured. Thus, every single member of the family of humanity is vital and must be kept and nurtured in our circle. Moreover, the knot is connected through a Wisdom knot, representing the Sophia of Christ (see Saint Hildutus) – we are all the people of God and united in his Wisdom made manifest in our Lord Jesus Christ. This Wisdom we find at the very heart of the cross, upon which our Lord gave his life that we might find Life in him, for it is through him that we are bound in love with one another and in the love of God the Almighty.

liturgy of the word

holy scripture

Now there are varieties of gifts, but the same Spirit; and there are varieties of service, but the same Lord; and there are varieties of working, but it is the same God who inspires them all in every one. To each is given the manifestation of the Spirit for the common good. To one is given through the Spirit the utterance of wisdom, and to another the utterance of knowledge according to the same Spirit, to another faith by the same Spirit, to another gifts of healing by the one Spirit, to another the working of miracles, to another prophecy, to another the ability to distinguish between spirits, to another various kinds of tongues, to another the interpretation of tongues. All these are inspired by one and the same Spirit, who apportions to each one individually as he wills.

For just as the body is one and has many members, and all the members of the body, though many, are one body, so it is with Christ. For by one Spirit we were all baptized into one body – Jews or Greeks, slaves or free – and all were made to drink of one Spirit. (1 Corinthians 12:4-13)

meditation

There is a great difference between a circle and a wheel. We usually see as our goal for humanity to have all people joined hand-in-hand in a great circle. And yet, the more people we can coax into the great circle, the farther apart we grow from one another. In the circle, we come into personal contact only with those immediately on our right and on our left, and when new people come into the circle next to us, they come between us and others we know.

Being in the circle of humanity can be a very frustrating experience. As more and more people join, we see those we had been close enough to talk with pushed ever farther away by new people. But we also want to talk with these new people and get to know them. In the circle, we simply cannot be close to everyone, although we approach the circle with that very desire: to join together with all of humanity.

Another problem with the circle of humanity is that it has no form. If we want the circle to move in one direction or another, we find that one section moves too quickly, another too slowly, and so the circle loses its shape and becomes distorted – perhaps it even breaks. Ideally, we would want the circle to move as a hoop; but if we try to stand it on end so that it might roll to its goal, the entire circle collapses into confusion, for there is nothing to keep the various members firmly enough in their positions within the circle to withstand the relentless pull of gravity.

What would make the circle better for the unity of all people? If there could be a way to connect with others wherever they may be on the circle – if we could all connect with everyone – then we would never suffer the frustration of being apart. If there could be a way to keep the circle from distorting and falling in upon itself, then we could all act in unity toward common goals for the good of all humanity.

What we need is for the circle to become a wheel – one with a hub and spokes. With the spokes connecting to everyone in the circle, we could all communicate through the hub. With the hub holding the spokes in place, our circle would become a rim, firm enough to stand on end and move as a single body.

The key, then, is the hub; and the hub is our Lord Jesus Christ. With Christ as the hub of the wheel, all who connect with him through the spokes of faith are connected with one another. We all become members of his one Body and Spirit. But more than this: If we maintain the spokes of faith firmly between Jesus and us, then the circle truly does become a wheel, capable of moving with speed and unity to whatever goal God may choose for us.

There is a great difference between a circle and a wheel, and the difference is the hub and the spokes. With Jesus as the hub and with the spokes of faith firmly connecting us to him from the many points on the rim, we are all in communion with one another and can work as one body in his unity; while without him, we become estranged from one another, and can never dwell together in unity. (Psalm 133)

liturgy of prayer

collect

Almighty and unifying God, who hast brought us together in the one Body and the one Spirit of our Lord and Savior Jesus Christ: Hold us in the unity of thine only true and adorable Son that we might all maintain the connection of love and faith with him and through him, and that all humanity might come together in unity and faith; through the same Jesus Christ our Lord, who liveth and reigneth with thee and the Holy Spirit, one God, for ever and ever. *Amen.*

hymn: the celtic cross

God, bind us together around thy dear Son,
that we may join to him and through him as one,
by faith in his Wisdom and trust in his Word
and loyalty to him as our only Lord.

With Christ at the center, we gather around
the hub of the wheel that is stable and sound.
We reach him with arms that like spokes hold us true,
our faith to affirm and our lives to renew.

In unity grasping to Jesus, we feel
the hands of our comrades across the great wheel,
each one of us bound to the other through him,
to whom we sing praises from out on the rim.

Now let us go forward, a wheel that will roll
throughout the wide earth to enlist every soul,
and growing to fill all the world with his Grace,
till finally we find thee and gaze on thy face.

thanksgiving

We thank thee, Lord, that thou hast given us the example of the Celtic Cross to guide us to a more perfect unity in thee.

grace

Almighty and everliving God, by thy Grace let us dwell together in the unity of the Cross.

The Celtic Cross

Stately

1. God, bind us to -
2. With Christ at the
3. In u - ni - ty
4. Now let us go

geth - er a - round thy dear
cen - ter, we ga - ther a -
grasp - ing to Je - sus, we
for - ward, a wheel that will

Son,   that   we   may   join
round   the   hub   of   the
feel   the   hands   of   our
roll   through -   out   the   wide

to   him   and   through   him   as
wheel   that   is   sta -   ble   and
com - rades a -   cross   the   great
earth   to   en -   list   eve - ry

one,   by   faith   in   his
sound.   We   reach   him   with
wheel, each   one   of   us
soul,   and   grow - ing   to

11

Wis-   dom   and   trust   in   his
arms   that   like   spokes   hold   us
bound   to   the   oth -   er   through
fill   all   the   world   with   his

Word   and   loy -   al -   ty
true,   our   faith   to   a -
him,   to   whom   we   sing
Grace,   till   fin -   ally   we

to   him   as   our   on -   ly
firm   and   our   lives   to   re -
prais -   es   from   out   on   the
find   thee   and   gaze   on   thy

12

Lord.
new.
rim.

face.

Saint Ita

A Celebration
of Quiet

january 15
---
commemoration of saint ita

saint ita

Second only to Saint Brigid among the most beloved of the Irish women saints, Saint Ita (also Ite and Ide) was born with the name Deirdre to the influential Deisi family. She died around the year 570 reputedly at a very old age at the nunnery she had founded in Killeedy, County Limerick.

Early in her ministry, she established a monastic school for boys. Her gentle ministry to them is reflected in the lullaby for the Infant Jesus that is attributed to her. The care and diligence with which she instructed them is attested in her description as the foster mother of the Irish saints, for so many of her boys were later proclaimed saints, including Saint Brendan.

The main characteristic she is remembered for, however, is the mystic indwelling of the Holy Trinity. The major turning points of her life are marked by visions and visitations by angels. These communions were achieved through rigorous asceticism and long periods of quiet solitude. There is even a story of an angel rebuking her for the extreme degree to which she would exercise these disciplines.

Certainly, she does not appear to have been well traveled, and she began her nunnery and school very early in life. The wisdom with which she managed her charges and taught the children was not derived from a classroom or from the tutelage of honored churchmen, nor was it gleaned from a life of active worldly experience. Rather, her insights were achieved through the quiet of solitary prayer and meditation.

the symbol

As Saint Ita saw it, there is only one way we can join our hearts with the love of Christ: We must take these hearts – our innermost thoughts and feelings – and move them ever more deeply into the heart of the cross. Thus, as the wheel of humanity is formed through Christ (through whom all things were made), we spiral from the outermost rim, where we dwell with our concerns about the world, ever urging our hearts to the center as we gradually replace our worldly thoughts and feelings with the desire for Wisdom. This centering prayer leads us to the heart of the cross. And in the heart of the cross we find our own hearts, for they too have been created by God, have been redeemed by Christ, and are continually sustained by the Holy Spirit.

liturgy of the word

holy scripture

And there he came to a cave, and lodged there;
and behold, the word of the LORD came to him, and

he said to him, "What are you doing here, Elijah?"
He said, "I have been very jealous for the LORD, the
God of hosts; for the people of Israel have forsaken
thy covenant, thrown down thy altars, and slain thy
prophets with the sword; and I, even I only, am left;
and they seek my life, to take it away." And he said,
"Go forth, and stand upon the mount before the
LORD." And behold, the LORD passed by, and a
great and strong wind rent the mountains, and
broke in pieces the rocks before the LORD, but the
LORD was not in the wind; and after the wind an
earthquake, but the LORD was not in the earthquake;
and after the earthquake a fire, but the LORD was
not in the fire; and after the fire a still small voice.
And when Elijah heard it, he wrapped his face in his
mantle and went out and stood at the entrance of
the cave. (I Kings 19:9-12)

meditation

Like Elijah, we expect God to appear to us in dramatic ways. We
look for the Lord in the wind, in the earthquake, in the fire. But if we
go to speak with God in the wind, we shall be consumed by the wind;
if we go to speak with God in the earthquake, we shall be consumed
by the earthquake; if we go to speak with God in the fire, we shall be
consumed by the fire. Only if we go to speak with God in silence, shall
we hear his voice.

The world is a noisy, tumultuous place – a place besieged by
chaos striving against the order of God's continuing Creation. Even
our own voices are accustomed to ranting and railing against one
another, and our ears are accustomed to the constant onslaught of
the tumult.

Our self-centered nature expects God to speak over the tumult –
over the chaos – to us. Of course, he loves us and wants to speak

with us, but God is not going to indulge us in our chaotic nature. He is the good Parent who does not pamper the spoiled child, but expects the child to listen, to be patiently attentive.

There are two reasons why it is not easy for us to listen: First, we want others – even God – to listen to us. Yet, we must be silent and listen not to what we want to hear, but to what God wants to tell us. Second, to listen we must prepare ourselves to hear. We must create a silent world around us, free of the distractions we love. And indeed we do love our distractions, for they save us from hearing things we are not prepared to heed.

When we shut out the chaos in the world, when we shut out the chaos in ourselves, we create the sheer silence in which we can hear God, for God speaks through a still small voice. We shut ourselves in a room and notice that a clock is ticking. We move away from the clock, and a cat jumps into our lap. We escape to a closet where there are no clocks, cats, or other distractions; but we are still not free, for rampaging through our heads are the many questions we have for God – and, of course, the preferred answers we hope God will give us.

It does not work this way.

But when, in those quite rare moments we can achieve sheer silence without and within, then the still small voice of God surrounds us with his message: It is as though he speaks without words through the very sound of silence.

Even then, the message is not what we want to hear. We want him to reveal himself to us, but he is not at our beck and call. We want him to address our problems and tell us precisely what to do, but God is the good Parent and will not do our thinking for us.

What God says is at once the most reassuring and the most frustrating thing He can say: Be patient; love and trust.

liturgy of prayer

collect

All knowing and yet all loving God, who speakest to us only when we are silent and only when we are willing to hear what thou wouldst tell us: Let our tongues be silent and our ears be shut and our minds be clear of the tumultuous world, that we might hear thy still small voice and learn what thou wouldst teach us; through Jesus Christ our Lord, who liveth and reigneth with thee and the Holy Spirit, one God, for ever and ever. *Amen.*

hymn: saint ita

REFRAIN   Let the wind blow,
let the earth shake,
let the fire glow.
Thy silence make.

In quiet solitude we seek
thy holy voice to hear,
keeping our thoughts subdued and meek
in silent awe and fear,

Let us hear what thy voice doth say
over the world's loud din.
Show us how quietly to pray
to let thy Spirit in.

Thy still small voice cannot be heard
in this tumultuous world,
where scornful laugh and spiteful word
are all too often hurled.

Thy Holy Word can we hear clear
only in quiet prayer.
So let us rest our thoughts and hear
what thou wouldst have us share.

thanksgiving

We thank thee, Lord, that thou dost give us the example of Saint Ita
to guide us to a more perfect quiet in thee.

grace

Almighty and everliving God, by thy Grace let us persevere in the quiet
of Ita.

Saint Ita

Serenely

Refrain Let the wind blow, blow,

let the earth shake,

let   the   fire   glow.

Thy   si -   lence   make.

1. In   qui -   et   sol -   it -
2. Let   us   hear   what   thy
3. Thy   still   small   voice   can -
4. Thy   Ho -   ly   Word   can

23

tude — we — seek
voice — doth — say
not — be — heard
we — hear — clear

thy — ho - ly — voice — to
o - ver — the — world's — loud
in — this — tu - — mult - — uous
on - — ly — in — qui - — et

hear,
din.
world,
prayer.

24

keep - ing our thoughts sub -
Show us how qui - et -
where scorn - ful laugh and
So let us rest our

dued and meek
ly to pray
spite - ful word
thoughts and hear

in si - lent awe and
to let thy Spir - it
are all too of - ten
what thou wouldst have us

25

fear.
in.
hurled.
share.

Repeat Refrain

Saint Maedoc

A Celebration

of Friendship

january 31
---
commemoration of
saint maedoc

saint maedoc

Saint Maedoc of Ferns (or Aedh or Aidan – Maedoc was a nickname from childhood meaning "my little Aedh") was born in Connacht and educated at Leinster. He traveled to Wales and studied at the school at St David's, where he learned the patterned and ascetic life that would manifest itself in later acts of austerity, such as fasting for seven years on bread and water and reciting 500 psalms every day. He returned to Leinster, and on land donated by Prince Bandrub, he founded the monastery at Ferns (County Wexford), where he served as abbot. He also founded monasteries at Drumlane and Rossinver. He died in the year 626.

For one who was noted for his acts of austerity, it may be a bit surprising that Saint Maedoc was best known for his generous and abiding friendship. There are many rather odd legends associated with the saint, including a prediction by the prophet Finn mac Cumaill that Maedoc would turn Ferns from a den of wolf cubs to a place of friendship. The reference to wolves was probably early and certainly intended to refer to humans, not to animals. Nonetheless, legends sprang up of Saint Maedoc's encountering wolves, feeding them, and making friends of them. There is no doubt that he had a pacifying influence over his region, offering friendship in place of that continuing enmity among people that had given rise to many feuds.

While envy and jealousy mar stories about the clergy's attitude toward the gracious Saint Ciaran of Clonmacnois, it was Saint Maedoc who sought him out and offered him the peace of friendship, establishing a close bond between his three monasteries and that of Clonmacnois. This trait of befriending everyone pervades the stories of his life and miracles, recognizing him as the good friend of saints, of the poor, of animals, and even of the dead.

When he himself was on his deathbed, one hundred fifty friends gathered around him and shared his last Eucharist with him. He bequeathed his bell, his staff, and his reliquary to his three beloved monasteries; and so great was the feeling of friendship and loyalty his monks had for him, that these three treasures were carefully preserved and survive today.

the symbol

The symbol of Saint Maedoc typifies the love of friends that we achieve in Christ. Within each heart is a form of Trinity knot, for the root of all human friendship is the loyalty and love given to us by the Holy Trinity. The love of friends connects the hearts within the love of the cross of Christ, in the very heart of which is the Wisdom knot – the loving Sophia of our Lord. We extend our friendship to one another as equals, represented in the fact that the arms of the cross are all of equal length – in Christ we are not ranked in friendship, but joined in Christian humility all on the same level.

liturgy of the word

holy scripture

"By this my Father is glorified, that you bear much fruit, and so prove to be my disciples. As the Father has loved me, so have I loved you; abide in my love. If you keep my commandments, you will abide in my love, just as I have kept my Father's commandments and abide in his love. These things I have spoken to you, that my joy may be in you, and that your joy may be full.

"This is my commandment, that you love one another as I have loved you. Greater love has no man than this, that a man lay down his life for his friends. You are my friends if you do what I command you. No longer do I call you servants, for the servant does not know what his master is doing; but I have called you friends, for all that I have heard from my Father I have made known to you. You did not choose me, but I chose you and appointed you that you should go and bear fruit and that your fruit should abide; so that whatever you ask the Father in my name, he may give it to you. This I command you. To love one another." (John 15:8-17)

meditation

We call many people our friends. We go to school with people we think of as very close friends and with whom we share some of the most important experiences of our lives. But then we grow up, we move apart; and our friends remain only as hazy shadows in our memory. From time to time we wonder whatever became of them; but now we have other, more pressing concerns, and we consign these friends to the past.

Of all of the people we come into contact with and drift apart from, how many are really friends? How many would we share our most intimate thoughts and feelings with? How many would we tell that deep dark secret to – the one that, if it were ever known, could destroy our lives? How many would we entrust with the dreams we have that are beyond our grasp?

When we ponder such questions, be begin to realize how truly lonely we are. With all the dreams and aspirations that are so important to our inner selves – that define who we are – we remain silent and alone. Is there no one in this world we can call a soul friend and with whom we can share our innermost being and our most important thoughts and feelings? The answer must be a deafening and defeating No – *unless* we are willing to enter into the innermost being and the most important thoughts and feelings of the friend with genuine interest and loving concern.

In our isolated and isolating human existence (and especially in these times of mobility and uncertainty), how can we possibly invest the emotional commitment in someone whom circumstance may take away from us at any moment? We are afraid of giving someone whom we may suddenly never see again true, deep, and abiding friendship.

Yct, we all have a Friend who made the supreme sacrifice of friendship for us. He died for us, so that we might live. He went through a most painful and humiliating death as a finite human being so that we might see the Way to eternal life. He died for us before we were even born: He was our Friend, passing on to us his most intimate thoughts and feelings and giving up his very life for us, and he never even met us.

If we indeed follow him in his commandment that we love one another, if we indeed follow him in his Way of love and sacrifice, then we shall see that we have had our questions about friendship turned around. Rather than waiting to find the "perfect" friend and the most

31

opportune circumstances for friendship, we should rather extend ourselves in friendship to everyone. We must first show a genuine interest and loving concern for the innermost being and the most important thoughts and feelings of others and also a willingness to share our souls with others.

As our culture tells us, to have a friend we must first be a friend. Of course, our culture speaks of conventional and rather shallow acts of friendship (albeit important acts, to be sure). Our Friend Christ, however, urges us in the same direction, but he requires that we deepen this friendship to the innermost level of our very souls, loving one another as he has loved us.

liturgy of prayer

collect

Almighty and yet most intimate God, who hast offered thyself in thine only Son our Lord as an act of eternal and steadfast love and friendship: Teach us through the example of Christ Jesus to treat one another as friends, that our souls may join in harmonious praise and thanksgiving to thee and that we never be lonely again; through the same Jesus Christ our Lord, who liveth and reigneth with thee and the Holy Spirit, one God, for ever and ever. *Amen.*

hymn: saint maedoc

The friendship of thy Son our Lord, oh God,
hast thou bequeathed us for all time –
a gift from One who on this earth hath trod
to know our inner souls sublime.

He did experience our joy and pain,
uncertainties of life and death,
and for our friendship he did not disdain
from offering his parting breath.

And lovingly to us did he command
that we should love the very same,
and give our friendship with an open hand
to everyone in Jesus' Name.

So let us join now all our souls as one
in friendship just as did our Lord,
in unity that cannot be undone;
oh, let us live in true accord.

thanksgiving

We thank thee, Lord, that thou has given us the example of Saint
Maedoc to guide us to a more perfect friendship in thee.

grace

Almighty and everliving God, by thy Grace let us love our friends with
the zeal of Maedoc.

Saint Maedoc

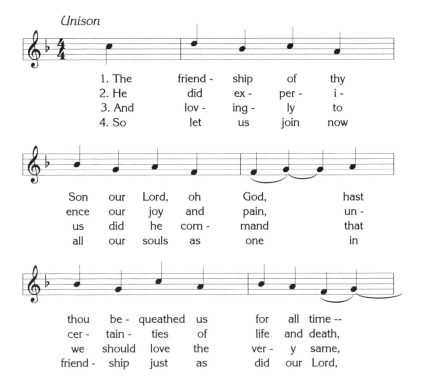

Unison

1. The friend - ship of thy
2. He did ex - per - i -
3. And lov - ing - ly to
4. So let us join now

Son our Lord, oh God, hast
ence our joy and pain, un -
us did he com - mand that
all our souls as one in

thou be - queathed us for all time --
cer - tain - ties of life and death,
we should love the ver - y same,
friend - ship just as did our Lord,

34

a   gift   from   One   who
and   for   our   friend -   ship
and   give   our   friend -   ship
in   u -   ni -   ty   that

on   earth   hast   trod   to
he   did   not   dis -   dain   from
with   an   o -   pen   hand   to
can -   not   be   un -   done;   oh,

know   our   in -   ner   souls   sub -   lime.
off -   er -   ing   his   part -   ing   breath.
eve -   ry -   one   in   Je -   sus'   Name.
let   us   live   in   true   ac -   cord.

Saint Brigid

A Celebration

of Love

februarζ 1

---

commemoration of saint brigiδ

saint brigiδ

Brigid (or Bridget, Briget, Bride) was a common name throughout the Celtic lands, and there were a number of saints who shared it. The one we think of most often is Saint Brigid of Ireland (who died around 525). She is one of the two patron saints of the whole of Ireland (the only native patron) and is said to have been baptized by the other patron, Saint Patrick, and to have been the abbess of Kildare.

Very little is known about Saint Brigid. All we have are collections of stories – most of them rather obviously formulaic and fanciful (such as the story of changing water into beer), and many of them probably originated with other saints or local figures (including a pagan goddess with the same popular name).

Two traits do stand out in the legends of Saint Brigid, however, and their prominence and frequency no doubt reflect a true recollection of the real saint. Time and time again she is cited for her great compassion and for maintaining the flame of Christianity in the darkness. The latter tradition is enhanced by stories of her nuns keeping sacred fires burning for long periods of time and by the fact that she has also become the patron of blacksmiths.

It is her compassion, though, that burns in our collective memory. Certainly, she was in charge of a most important abbey and had much authority over what was in all probability a rather large region. And yet, she would welcome sojourners and strangers into her cloister home. During the tumultuous period of the Dark Ages,

38

strangers were usually looked upon with suspicion, and sojourners would often turn out to be robbers or pirates. So her deeds of compassion were not without considerable risk to herself.

Above all, she would feed the hungry, minister to the sick, and support the poor. It was this care for the hungry, the sick, the poor – those living on the margins of society in a dangerous world – that lives on as the real character of Saint Brigid of Ireland. She envisioned a great feast of love and kindness at the Table of our Lord, to which she would invite the hungry to eat and the sick to dance.

Thus, she becomes for us the embodiment of the Steadfast Love that God shows his people both in the Hebrew Scriptures and in the Christian Testament. The Hebrew prophets constantly reminded a wayward people of their need to care for those living on the margins of Jewish society, for these were indeed the people of God. Jesus emphatically reiterates this need for compassion – compassion for all people everywhere.

Saint Brigid is the model of compassion and caring for others within the Steadfast Love of God. Whatever she was and whatever she had she dedicated to the love and care of God's children.

the symbol

The wheel of the cross is fashioned into a heart, representing the love of Christ on the cross. The heart, though, is a knot, holding within itself a three-part loop of the Trinity, just as Saint Brigid held the love of the Trinity within her heart and made it an integral part of her heart. The cross is the traditional cross of Saint Brigid, usually made up of strands of straw, showing the humility of her love. Each strand of her cross grasps through other strands and holds onto a strand in the next group. In this we can visualize four right hands, each grasping the wrist of another person to the right. Thus, the love that binds the people of God together turns ever around upon the heart of the love of the Trinity.

liturgy of the word

holy scripture

"For it will be as when a man going on a journey called his servants and entrusted to them his property; to one he gave five talents, to another two, to another one, to each according to his ability. Then he went away. He who had received the five talents went at once and traded with them; and he made five talents more. So too, he who had the two talents made two talents more. But he who had received the one talent, went and dug in the ground and hid his master's money. Now after a long time the master of those servants came and settled accounts with them. And he who had received the five talents came forward, bringing five talents more, saying. 'Master, you delivered to me five talents; here I have made five talents more.' His master said to him, 'Well done, good and faithful servant; you have been faithful over a little, I will set you over much; enter into the joy of your master.' And he also who had the two talents came forward, saying. 'Master, you delivered to me two talents; here I have made two talents more.' His master said to him, 'Well done, good and faithful servant; you have been faithful over a little, I will set you over much; enter into the joy of your master.' He also who had received the one talent came forward, saying, 'Master, I knew you to be a hard man, reaping where you did not sow, and gathering where you did not winnow; so I was afraid, and I went and hid your talent in the ground. Here you have what is yours.' But his master answered him, 'You wicked and slothful servant! You know that I reap where I have not sowed and gather where I have not winnowed. Then you ought to have invested my money with the bankers, and at my coming I should have received what was my own with interest. So take the talent from him, and give it to him who has the ten talents. For to every one who has will more be given, and he will have abundance; but from him who has not, even what he has will be taken away. And cast the worthless servant into the outer darkness; there men will weep and gnash their teeth.'"(Matthew 25:14-30)

meditation

Let us imagine ourselves as the "wicked and slothful servant" who has received the one talent, for that is who we truly are in this parable of Jesus. And the lord is indeed the Lord God.

We are confused and distressed. The other servants have done more than we have, to be sure, and they are getting their reward. But have we not preserved what the Lord has given us? The Lord gave us a talent – a considerable amount of money – and we have guarded it and kept it safe for his return. Now he is angry with us and casts us into the outer darkness, away from his Light.

We feel the perspiration on our foreheads, our knees wobble, our hands feel as though they carry the weight of the world. What have we done to deserve such condemnation? We feel angry, trapped, and betrayed. There must be some mistake, but we know that the Lord cannot make a mistake. Are we to be condemned simply for not increasing the talent he gave to us for safe keeping?

The talents God has given us are our hearts. Those who have a great heart do not keep it to themselves, but they lend it out in acts of love; and the greater the acts of love they show, the greater is the love of their fellow humanity that flows back to them.

But we who have only one small heart are afraid. What if we were to extend our single heart to one of God's children who was hungry, sick, or poor, and that person were to reject us? Should we therefore not guard and protect our one single heart from harm?

When we think this way, we forget that it was the Lord himself who gave us this heart with the hope that we would share it with others. For it is only through sharing the Steadfast Love of God that it will increase and bring the Kingdom of heaven to earth. We cannot receive the Steadfast Love of God and then fail to pass it on. As Jesus constantly reminds us, there are really only two commandments – two things that are expected of us to enter into a relationship of love with God and likewise with each other: "You shall love the Lord your God with all your heart, and with all your soul, and with all your mind. This is the great and first commandment. And a second is like it, You shall love your neighbor as yourself. On these two commandments depend all the law and the prophets." (Matthew 22:37b-40).

The servant with the one talent – with the one heart that he dare not put into jeopardy – does not really love his lord with all of this heart. For to love his lord is to love his lord's people, including those who may be dangerous or unreceptive. After all, God offers us his love with no conditions and offers us his help and his Grace with no expectations.

Let us not forget Jesus' words to Saint Peter: "When they had finished breakfast, Jesus said to Simon Peter 'Simon, son of John, do you love me more than these?' He said to him, 'Yes, Lord; you know that I love you.' He said to him, 'Feed my lambs.'" (John 21:15).

collect

Almighty and all loving God, who bestowest upon us thy Steadfast Love by thine eternal and all-encompassing Grace: Grant that we may have the courage and the will not only to accept thy loving kindness, but to pass on thy Holy Spirit to all thy people, and above all to the hungry, the sick, and the poor who depend upon us to be reflections of thy great mercy; through Jesus Christ our Lord, who liveth and reigneth with thee and the Holy Spirit, one God, for ever and ever. *Amen.*

hymn: saint brigid

Oh Lord, we look to thee for Grace
before thy throne enthralled,
but when we see a human face
we look away appalled

by hunger's gaunt and hollow shell,
by poverty's despair,
by malady's abysmal well,
by danger's dreaded lair.

When will we learn to share our hearts
as thou hast given thine –
and not in timid, fitful starts,
but boldly as a sign

of that great Love for us thou hast,
as freely thou didst give
in pain thine only Son at last
to die that we might live?

thanksgiving

We thank thee, Lord, that thou hast given us the example of Saint Brigid to guide us to a more perfect love in thee.

grace

Almighty and everliving God, by thy Grace let love thee and one another with the intensity of Brigid.

Saint Brigid

1. Oh   Lord,   we
2. When   will   we

look   to   thee   for
learn   to   share   our

Grace be - fore thy
hearts as thou hast

throne en - thralled,
giv - en thine --

but when we
and not in

46

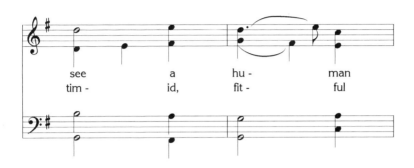

see   a   hu -   man
tim -   id,   fit -   ful

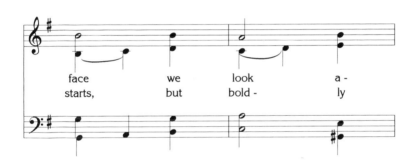

face   we   look   a -
starts,   but   bold -   ly

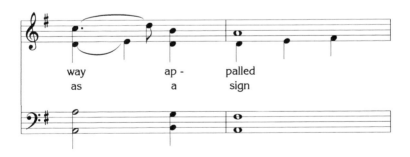

way   ap -   palled
as   a   sign

47

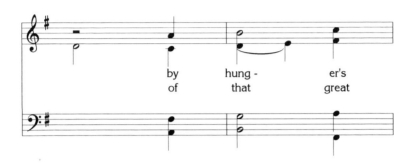

by   hung -   er's
of   that   great

gaunt   and   hol -   low
Love   for   us   thou

shell,   by   pov -   er -
hast,   as   free -   ly

48

ty's   des -   pair,
thou   didst   give

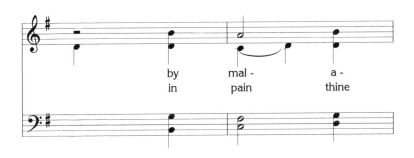

      by   mal -   a -
      in   pain   thine

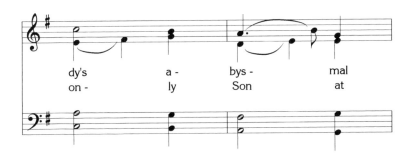

dy's   a -   bys -   mal
on -   ly   Son   at

49

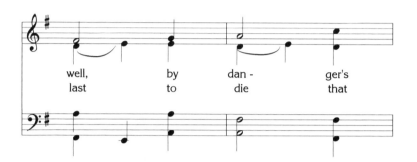

well,   by   dan -   ger's
last   to   die   that

dread -   ded   lair.
we   might   live?

Saint David

A Celebration
of Inspiration

march 1
---
commemoration of
saint david

saint david

Saint David (Dewi or Dafydd in Welsh) was born at the beginning of the sixth century and died near the end of it. The patron saint of Wales, he was Bishop of Menevia and established churches throughout South Wales and as far away as Cornwall and Brittany. For his time, this was a considerable range indeed.

Very little reliable information can be found about his life. He had the nickname *Aquaticus* 'Waterman' perhaps for several reasons: He instituted a strict prohibition on alcoholic drinks among his clergy (according to the oldest, but not necessarily the most reliable tradition), he spread the Gospel along the water routes of the Celtic Church (his churches in Cornwall and Brittany might suggest this), he immersed himself in cold water as a means of discipline and mortification of the flesh (another old tradition reflecting a widespread practice), he exercised the rite of Baptism to a remarkable degree (and indeed there was some dispute on this between the British and the Roman Churches), or he made use of the old sacred wells, converting them to Christian use (a well documented practice reaching even into the twentieth century).

There was one miracle associated with Saint David that bears close examination. At an episcopal synod in Brefi, there was a heated debate among the various bishops on an important matter – probably having to do with the penitentials, less likely concerning a popular heresy. Whatever the issue was, Saint David was only one among many bishops in the loud assembly.

Suddenly the Holy Spirit inspired Saint David. He spoke with such eloquence and authority that the entire synod hushed and turned to him, listening to his message from the Holy Trinity. In later accounts, the miracle was described as the ground rising up under the saint and lifting him above the crowd so that they might hear God's message.

More likely, it was the inspired eloquence and the aura of divine authority that elevated him above the petty concerns of the arguers. It was as though a mountain rose up beneath him as he spoke. Indeed, in the metaphorical language of the age, a mountain did rise up beneath him, enabling him to speak, as it were, from the mountaintop in the tradition of Moses in the Exodus and also of Jesus in his Sermon on the Mount (which Saint Matthew may well be using metaphorically as well – compare Saint Luke's Sermon on the Plain).

No matter how we wish to interpret what happened on that day, one fact is clear: By the miracle of the inspiration of God through the Holy Spirit, Saint David became the spokesman of God for his people and for all the people of God.

the symbol

As Saint David was lifted by the inspiration of God to proclaim the divine Word, so is the cross in this symbol thrust up through the mountain by the knot of the Holy Trinity. The mountain itself is topped by the wheel of humanity, for we are all creatures of the earth. The power of God, however, is far greater than the power of the earth, and the cross blossoms through humanity by the power of the Spirit. This cross is based upon the traditional cross of Saint David, with the mountain at the foot and three Trinitarian lines (here fashioned into a form of Trinity knot) coming off the head and arms. Thus, we see that the Holy Trinity expresses its very essence through acts of Grace in the world and in spite of any opposition the world may offer.

liturgy of the word

holy scripture

"And when they bring you before the synagogues and the rulers and the authorities, do not be anxious how or what you are to answer or what you are to say; for the Holy Spirit will teach you in that very hour what you ought to say." (Luke 12:11-12)

First of all you must understand this, that no prophecy of scripture is a matter of one's own interpretation, because no prophecy ever came by the impulse of man, but men moved by the Holy Spirit spoke from God. (2 Peter 1:20-21)

meditation

How often we have stood in a crowd of people and wanted desperately for them to listen to us! We had something very important on our minds, but everyone else just went on talking and jostling, going about their business without the slightest regard for us.

We see this often with little children who have pestered their parents to the point that the parents just will not listen. The children jump up and down, wave their arms, call relentlessly to their parents over and over again. We can see on their faces that what they have to say at that very moment has become the most important communication in their young lives.

Perhaps we have listened to a discussion on the radio and have called the station to express our opinion only to find that the lines are all busy with other people calling in with their opinions. Do they not know that our opinion is very important and needs to be heard?

Whenever we have something important to say and no one bothers to listen, we feel small, insignificant, and alone. We have no friends – we have been abandoned by everyone we thought we knew. Everyone is far more interested in someone else. But we know we have the answer. We know we have the most important piece of information, the most important opinion. In a word: We are totally frustrated.

Is it really so important though – our opinion about a political candidate, our concern with the logic of someone we disagree with, our plans for expanding and beautifying our church? Of course, such matters are important to us at the moment; but do we really possess the most crucial pieces of information or opinions on the most important matter?

And what is the most important matter if it is not establishing the Kingdom of God? Here again, we may well be ready to leap into the fray and shout our opinions and plans for bringing God's Kingdom to earth. And once again, it may well be that no one will listen to us.

Let us rest assured, however, that if we do in fact have the most important insight into this most important matter, it will not have come from us, but it will have been inspired by God through the Holy Spirit. And if indeed the Holy Spirit speaks through us, it will be as though a mountain were raised beneath our feet. The assembly will become awesomely quiet and listen as they have never listened before.

Perhaps this, then, is the lesson we should learn when we try desperately to get people's attention and make them listen to us but they ignore what we have to say: Although we may believe we speak the truth above all truths, we can say nothing of such importance unless the Holy Spirit flows through us and inspires us to proclaim the Word of God. Until then, we are but one voice among many in a deafening din.

liturgy of prayer

collect

Almighty and all inspiring God, who causest us to speak with the
tongue of the Holy Spirit whenever it serveth thy purpose for us: Grant
us the eloquence to convince others of what is right in thy sight, and
grant us the wisdom to know and accept the difference between thy
speaking through us and our speaking presumptuously for thee;
through Jesus Christ our Lord, who liveth and reigneth with thee and
the Holy Spirit, one God, for ever and ever. *Amen.*

hymn: saint david

Grant us a tongue that we might speak
what thou wouldst have us say,
for our own words too often seek
to justify our way.

Vanity mocketh thy great Word,
and bringeth us to boast
not of thy saving Grace, oh Lord,
but of ourselves the most.

For inspiration, Lord, we pray –
thy holy breath of life –
that we receive the Word to say
that endeth human strife.

thanksgiving

We thank thee, Lord, that thou hast given us the example of Saint David to guide us to a more perfect inspiration in thee.

grace

Almighty and everliving God, by thy Grace let us be filled with the inspiration of David.

Saint David

speak   what   thou   wouldst
Word   and   bring -   eth
pray --   thy   ho -   ly

have   us   say,
us   to   boast
breath   of   life --

for   our   own
not   of   thy
that   we   re -

59

words   too   of -   ten
sav -   ing   Grace,   oh
ceive   the   Word   to

seek   to   just -   i -
Lord,   but   of   our -
say   that   end -   eth

fy   our   way
selves   the   most.
hu -   man   strife

60

Saint Nonna

A Celebration

of Tenacity

march 3
(june 25 at alternon)
---
commemoration of saint nonna

saint nonna

Very little is known about the late-fifth-century Saint Nonna (or Nonnita – in Welsh, Non) other than the fact that she was the mother of Saint David, Patron of Wales. She herself, however, is more closely connected with Altarnon in Cornwall, where a church and a well are dedicated to her. Her tomb lies in Dirinon in Brittany, where she died.

Her strong connections in the three British Celtic lands – with dedications in Wales, Cornwall, and Brittany – suggest that she was an important saint in her own right and not simply the mother of a major patron. Evidently, she was a nun at least in the latter part of her life and may well have been a member of the religious community when Saint David was born, as celibacy was not a mark of many orders in the Celtic Church.

The later legends show confusion on this last point, since to those writing them down in the medieval church celibacy was very much a factor, and the birth of Saint David had to be accommodated somehow. Some legends claim that she was a nun ravished by someone named Sant; but this explanation is too formulaic for mothers of major figures. Such stories attempt rather clumsily to show that the mother had not willingly conceived and was therefore pure, as was the Virgin Mary. The name *Sant* 'Saint' likewise arouses suspicions.

The alternative story that she was the daughter of a powerful chieftain of the area around what is now St David's in Dyfed seems far more likely, given her importance in a wide area. At that time, the chief saints were often from the ruling families of Britain, and her membership in the "nobility" would certainly afford her movement between Wales, Cornwall, and Brittany.

At this point, a pervasive and tenacious legend enters the picture – one that is so persistent that it may well contain some factual basis. When she was pregnant with Saint David, for some reason she was out alone along the coast of Dyfed, on the peninsula now called St David's Head – on the very edge of Wales. As some legends would have it, she was exiled from her home, perhaps because she was with child against the wishes of her family.

On the eve of the first of March, a storm came crashing in from the sea. Such storms in that area are ferocious and terrifying, with waves breaking violently on the cliffs and coursing over them. Pelted by rain and whipped by fierce winds, she clung to a rock throughout the night. In the morning, the sun rose and her child was born. There is still a rock standing there with indentations claimed to have been made by Nonna's hands. A short distance away is St David's Cathedral.

the symbol

The symbol of Saint Nonna is a rock, with two indentations on the sides, representing the grasp the saint maintained on that rock. The rock itself is the Rock of Christ – the unswerving faith in his Word to which Saint Peter (whose name means 'the rock') and Saint Nonna clung so tenaciously. Within the rock is the Trinity knot, the never-ending connectedness of God the Creator, the Redeemer, the Sustainer – all of one essence. Upon this rock is the cross of the Celtic Church, being also of one essence with the rock itself. Thus it is that our tenacious grasp on the rock of faith is inspired by the Trinity and is both what makes up Christ's Holy Church and what holds it up as well.

liturgy of the word

holy scripture

When we cry. "Abba! Father!" it is the Spirit himself bearing witness with our spirit that we are children of God, and fellow heirs with Christ, provided we suffer with him in order that we may also be glorified with him.

    I consider that the sufferings of this present time are not worth comparing with the glory that is to be revealed to us. For the creation waits with eager longing for the revealing of the sons of God; for the creation was subjected to futility, not of its own will but by the will of him who subjected it in hope; because the creation itself will be set free from its bondage to decay and obtain the glorious liberty of the children of God We know that the whole creation has been groaning in travail together until now; and not only the creation, but we ourselves, who have the first fruits of the Spirit, groan inwardly as we wait for adoption as sons, the redemption of our bodies. (Romans 8:15-23)

meditation

We stand upon a cliff and suffer the fierce winds and driving rains of the sea – identified from the time of the Hebrew Scriptures as the Chaos. This is a world that is not yet Created, and we stand in the midst of it. Waves crash into the rocks below, deafening us so that we cannot hear what we try to shout to one another. Rain pelts our eyes, blinding us so that we cannot see one another. Cold winds enwrap our bodies, numbing us so that we cannot feel ourselves or the ground around us or the rocks we cling to.

How easy it would be to let go of the rocks and finally succumb to the Chaos. We have reached the point at which death would be a welcome release from all our suffering at the frigid hands of the storm. We cry out for help, but no one hears us. We look for salvation, but we can see only water and doom.

Yet in the midst of the trial of Chaos, God is effecting his Creation. If we can only make it through this night, the dawn will bring peace and salvation, wholeness and redemption. We know the Light always follows the painful acts of Creation out of Chaos, but how hard it is to hold onto the rocks.

This is life. The forces of Chaos constantly assault us with disasters of nature, plots of humans, failures of will. One catastrophe after another greets us, as our families and friends turn on us or depart from us, our neighbors bring suits against us or spread slanders about us, our employers let us go and our creditors demand payment. We cry out in anguish that life is over and there is no hope of going on.

This is when we must cling for Life to the eternal Rock – the faith of our Lord Jesus Christ. Here let us be precise in our Hebrew and Christian tradition: Throughout the Bible, God is faithful to us, even when we are not faithful to him. It is not a matter of our faith in Jesus, but of his faith in us that will bring us to the dawn.

Here we remember the trials of Saint Peter – Saint Peter who was always saying or doing the wrong thing, who denied his Savior three times before the cock crowed. Poor, battered Saint Peter clung tenaciously to the Rock through trial after trial, holding firmly to his salvation through the Lord. This is the tenacity that caused Jesus to name him *Petros* 'rock': "And I tell you, you are Peter, and on this rock I will build my church, and the powers of death shall not prevail against it" (Matthew 16:18).

And so we cling to the Rock and wait for the dawn.

liturgy of prayer

collect

All creating God, who hast tenaciously kept faith in us in spite of our faithlessness and hast given us a Rock to which we may cling through all the trials of Chaos that vainly seek to halt thy Creation: Grant us strength of will and tenacity of spirit that we may grip the Rock of our salvation neither despairing nor slipping, but ever hoping and holding; through Jesus Christ our Lord, who liveth and reigneth with thee and the Holy Spirit, one God, for ever and ever. *Amen.*

hymn: saint nonna

Let the storm rage around us and darkness descend,
let the Chaos unleash all its might,
for we cling to a Rock that will ever defend
us until we break into the Light.

In Creation we seek the Almighty's reward
who hath promised to show us the Path,
if we only can hold to his infinite Word
persevering through Chaos' dark wrath.

So we cling to the Rock and we wait for the dawn,
giving all of our trust to the Lord,
knowing his trust in us never will be withdrawn,
for on that hath he given his Word.

Let us cling to the Rock for the dawn cometh nigh
and the terror of Chaos will end.
Let us cling to the Rock, let us look to the sky,
let us trust in our Christ, in our Friend.

thanksgiving

We thank thee, Lord, that thou hast given us the example of Saint
Nonna to guide us to a more perfect tenacity in thee.

grace

Almighty and everliving God, by thy Grace let us be as tenacious in
our faith as was Nonna.

Saint Nonna

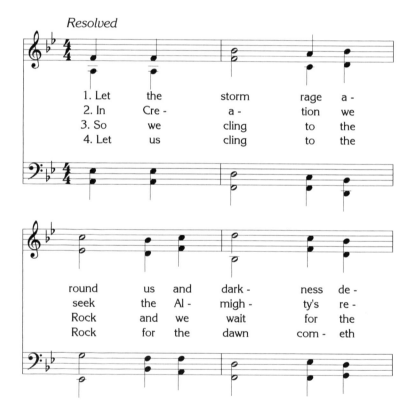

Resolved

1. Let the storm rage a -
2. In Cre - a - tion we
3. So we cling to the
4. Let us cling to the

round us and dark - ness de -
seek the Al - migh - ty's re -
Rock and we wait for the
Rock for the dawn com - eth

scend, let the Cha- os un-
ward who hath prom- ised to
dawn, giv- ing all of our
nigh and the ter- ror of

leash all its might,
show us the Path,
trust to the Lord,
Cha- os will end.

for we cling to a
if we on- ly can
know- ing his trust in
Let us cling to the

Rock that will ev - er de -
hold to his in - fin - ite
us nev - er will be with -
Rock, let us look to the

fend us un - til we break
Word per - sev - er - ing through
drawn, for on that hath he
sky, let us trust in our

in - to the Light.
Cha - os' dark wrath.
giv - en his Word.
Christ, in our Friend.

70

Saint Patrick

A Celebration
of Forgiveness

march 17
---
commemoration of saint patrick

saint patrick

Of all the Celtic saints, none is as famous or as widely beloved as Saint Patrick, who lived from about 390 to about 461. Nor is any life of a Celtic saint as well known, for he has left us his *Confessions*, a profoundly moving work that gives us insights not only into the life of the Saint, but also into the twilit world of the Dark Ages. Along with this autobiography, we have a letter to a British leader Coroticus and the famous *Lorica*, or Saint Patrick's Breastplate (and although this last work is of disputed authorship, it is clearly within his spirit). These are the first writings firmly identifiable as coming from the Celtic Church.

He was born in western Britain either in Wales or in regions whose people would migrate to Wales in the ensuing centuries of English domination. Although his father was prominent in the Romano-British magisterium as a town councillor and was certainly active in the Church as a deacon (as his father had been active before him – the Priest Potitus), the young Patrick must not have taken either his civic responsibilities or his church membership very seriously, for he later wrote, albeit in elegant and rhetorically well-formed Latin, that he lacked education, had turned away from God, and had failed to keep God's commandments.

The event that turned his life around came at about age sixteen: He was captured by a band of Gaelic pirates, who brought him as a slave to Ireland. For six years he worked as a shepherd without the slightest hope of escaping the farm, much less of crossing the Irish

Sea back home to Britain. But one night he heard a voice telling him to leave at once and go to the shore, where he would find a boat ready to sail. Although he did not know the way, he followed the Voice of God and was saved.

In Britain, he was again captured by pagans and saved by God. Finally, he saw the image of a man named Victoricus in a dream. Victoricus was coming from Ireland with many letters – one for Patrick. In the dream, the saint opened the letter and found a plea from the Irish people to return and to show them the Way of Christ. Thus it was that Saint Patrick, who had learned the Irish language in captivity, returned to Ireland to use his knowledge of the language and his renewed relationship of faith in God to preach to his former captors.

As missionary and bishop in Ireland, Saint Patrick grew to see his former enemies and captors as his friends and his flock. Indeed, he has come to be one of the two patron saints of Ireland – the other being Saint Brigid. The forgiving love he showed to his oppressors can be seen most clearly in his letter to his fellow Briton Coroticus, whom he rebukes for having slain some Irish pilgrims Patrick had converted.

Clearly, here was a man who knew the true meaning of forgiveness – forgiveness that goes beyond one's friends and family and extends to one's oppressors and enemies. Surely here too is an overwhelming faith in God, for Saint Patrick showed blind trust in his Lord to deliver him from and then to deliver him to those who were to become people of God.

the symbol

Within this simple, unadorned, and even cross is the Trinity knot, representing Saint Patrick's devotion to the Three in One, the One in Three. Legend has it that Saint Patrick described the Trinity through a shamrock, in which the leaves were separate but were made up all of the same essence and deriving from the same holy stem. Thus, God is the Creator of our souls, the Redeemer of our souls, and the Sustainer of our souls, appearing to us in these three different roles; and yet he is always the same God. The Trinity knot also portrays this concept, but without the stem – the roles of God are all interconnected and never-ending. This particular Trinity knot is composed of three Trinity knots, connecting the center with the outer edges along the rim of the wheel. Thus, God reaches out from his innermost essence through his three and many roles to touch our lives in every way. The interconnection of the Trinity knots also creates a significant image, for as the roles of God interconnect to join him with us, they form hearts reminiscent of God's Steadfast Love for his people.

liturgy of the word

holy scripture

"But I say to you that hear, Love your enemies, do good to those who hate you, bless those who curse you, pray for those who abuse you. To him who strikes you on the cheek, offer the other also; and from him who takes away your cloak do not withhold your coat as well. Give to every one who begs from you; and of him who takes away your goods, do not ask them again. And as you wish that men would do to you, do so to them.

"If you love those who love you, what credit is that to you? For even sinners love those who love them. And if you do good to those who do good to you, what credit is that to you? For even sinners do the same. And if you lend to those from whom you hope to receive, what credit is that to you? Even sinners lend to sinners, to receive as much again. But love your enemies, and do good, and lend, expecting nothing in return; and your reward will be great, and you will be sons of the Most High; for he is kind to the ungrateful and the selfish. Be merciful, even as your Father is merciful." (Luke 6:27-36)

But now in Christ Jesus you who once were far off have been brought near in the blood of Christ. For he is our peace, who has made us both one, and has broken down the dividing wall of hostility, by abolishing in his flesh the law of commandments and ordinances, that he might create in himself one new man in place of the two, so making peace, and might reconcile us both to God in one body through the cross, thereby bringing the hostility to an end. And he came and preached peace to you who were far off and peace to those who were near; for through him we both have access in one Spirit to the Father. So then you are no longer strangers and sojourners, but you are fellow citizens with the saints and members of the household of God, built upon the foundation of the apostles and prophets, Christ Jesus himself being the chief cornerstone, in whom the whole structure is joined together and grows into a holy temple in the Lord; in whom you also are built into it for a dwelling place of God in the Spirit. (Ephesians 2:13-22)

meditation

We have been wronged. There is no one on earth who cannot make that statement. And as assuredly as it is made, it is accompanied by bitter memory and the burning desire to make things right – to wreak vengeance upon our enemies and our oppressors.

Perhaps the wrong was committed against us personally, and we feel an immediate need to strike back and to show that we cannot be intimidated. Perhaps the wrong was committed against our people in some far away place, and we feel the need to support them by attacking their enemies who are doing the wrong – or maybe even the relatives of the enemies who happen by chance to be near us, even if they have no desire to harm anyone. Perhaps the wrong was committed long ago against our ancestors, and we feel the need to take revenge upon the descendants of their oppressors, even if they have done no harm themselves.

But what if, after exercising our vengeance however justly we perceive it, we look hard into the eyes of our enemy? What will we see? Is it not the same bitter memory and burning desire to set things right that we experienced ourselves? For our enemy is not a monster, but a human being just like us. If we take revenge and we look into our enemy's eyes, we will see ourselves.

We are so fond of proclaiming the Law of Retribution: "Eye for eye, tooth for tooth" (Exodus 21:24a), that we forget that even this law was established by God to limit retribution in an attempt to stop the spiral of vengeance. And of course, we forget entirely the words of our Lord Jesus Christ who gives us the highest law: "Love your enemies, do good to those who hate you."

The next time we want to take vengeance, let us imagine the face of Christ between our face and the face of our enemy. How is he looking at us? Do we see the pain in his face? Do we see how his face becomes one with that of our enemy? For he is indeed the Savior not just of us, our clan, and our nation; he is the Savior of the whole world – and he includes our enemies among his dearly beloved flock, whether they profess to believe in him or not (for he indeed believes in them). Can we really strike back at an enemy who bears the face of Jesus, painfully longing for us to give him that same forgiveness that he showed us before we were even born?

Only when we see the face of Jesus in our enemy, will we see the face of Jesus in ourselves.

liturgy of prayer

collect

All loving and forgiving God, who by thy great mercy hast shown us the Way in our Lord Jesus Christ to give mercy: Grant that we may so radiate thy love and forgiveness that no more should people hate one another but see thy face in the face of all thy people; through the same Jesus Christ our Lord, who liveth and reigneth with thee and the Holy Spirit, one God, for ever and ever. *Amen.*

hymn: saint patrick

Although Christ Jesus knoweth all manner of man
and all manner of woman too,
he perceiveth not in us what base humans can:
He perceiveth not state nor hue.

Though the nations engage in their bloodsoaking war
and enslave with the coin and sword,
our Lord Jesus commandeth we stand and implore
them to peace through his precious Word.

Could we only forgive and forget all that we
have endured from our enemy,
then we could look beyond all their faces and see
the compassionate face of thee.

thanksgiving

We thank thee, Lord, that thou has given us the example of Saint
Patrick to guide us to a more perfect forgiveness in thee.

grace

Almighty and everliving God, by thy Grace let us forgive one another
as Patrick forgave even his enemies.

Saint Patrick

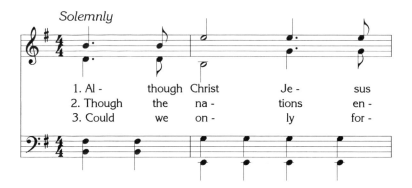

Solemnly

1. Al - though Christ Je - sus
2. Though the na - tions en -
3. Could we on - ly for -

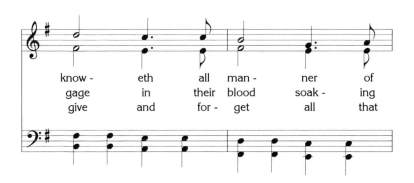

know - eth all man - ner of
gage in their blood soak - ing
give and for - get all that

man and all man - ner of
war and en - slave with of the
we have en - dured from our

wom - an too,
coin and sword,
en - em - y,

he per - ceiv - eth not
our Lord Je - sus com -
then we could look be -

80

in   us   what base   hu -   mans
mand - eth   we   stand   and   im -
yond   all   their fac -   es   and

can: He   per - ceiv -   eth   not
plore them   to   peace   through his
see   the   com - pas -   sion -   ate

1.-2.

state   nor   hue.
prec -   ious   Word.

81

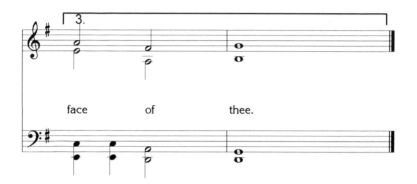

face   of   thee.

Saint Beuno

A Celebration

of Healing

april 21

---

commemoration of saint beuno

saint beuno

The most famous of the Cambrian "local saints" was Saint Beuno, a sixth-century abbot in North Wales. He was evidently born and raised around Hereford, where he doubtless came under the influence of the traditions of Saint Dubricius. His main work though was in the monastery he founded at Clynnog Fawr in Gwynedd. While there are other dedications to him in the region, some of these may have been established by his disciples in his name. There are many legends surrounding him, some including a miraculous coat that could not be made wet, the symbolism and religious significance of which has unfortunately become too vague to offer us any insights now.

As always when we look at the life of a Celtic saint, we are drawn to the most persistent and pervasive story, in order to gain the most reliable insights into who he was and what he did. For Saint Beuno, this is clearly the legend that he raised six people from the dead and would raise a seventh. With our modern techniques, medications, and equipment, we are still awed when someone who has lost all outward signs of life is "brought back." In the Dark Ages, only a saint with the Grace of God could possess such healing powers as to accomplish this feat through little else than prayer, faith, and loving care.

Perhaps the most prominent story involves a maiden, later known as Saint Winefride (or Gwenfrewi in Welsh) – a niece of Beuno's, who was fleeing from a nobleman's amorous advances. She ran to Saint Beuno's monastery, only to be caught at the last step by the nobleman, who rather than losing his prey drew his sword and dealt her a mortal blow. With her head reportedly severed (or more likely, her throat deeply slit), she lay lifeless in front of the saint's door. The saintly healer took her up, cared for her wound, and continued the Eucharist he had been celebrating – now mingling his prayers and concerns for her with the service of thanksgiving for life. And she lived.

This is the classic model of a Celtic saint's miracle. Alone, Saint Beuno's prayers could not have closed the gaping wound; nor alone could the scant healing powers of his age have brought her back. It took both the divine and the human – the faith in God's Grace and the hands of a healer – to work the miracle.

the symbol

A saintly miracle occurs when the Holy Spirit of the Trinity interacts with the caring heart of the human to affect the people of God within the love of Christ. All of these elements are needed in the measure ordained by God. Thus, the symbol of Saint Beuno the Healer represents the healing that flows from the Trinity knot with the Holy Spirit through the heart of the caring healer and into the circle of humanity. This healing process is intertwined with the cross of our Lord Jesus Christ, who gave himself that our spirits might also be healed. Healing, after all, leads to wholeness; and as the act of healing involves both the spiritual love and the caring hand, so the wholeness of health involves both the spirit and the body.

liturgy of the word

holy scripture

Now a certain man was ill, Lazarus of Bethany, the village of Mary and her sister Martha. It was Mary who anointed the Lord with ointment and wiped his feet with her hair, whose brother Lazarus was ill. So the sisters sent to him, saying, "Lord, he whom you love is ill." But when Jesus heard it he said, "This illness is not unto death; it is for the glory of God, so that the Son of God may be glorified by means of it."

. . .

Now when Jesus came, he found that Lazarus had already been in the tomb four days.

. . .

Then Mary, when she came where Jesus was and saw him, fell at his feet, saying to him, "Lord, if you had been here, my brother would not have died." When Jesus saw her weeping, and the Jews who came with her also weeping, he was deeply moved in spirit and troubled; and he said, "Where have you laid him?" They said to him, "Lord, come and see." Jesus wept. So the Jews said, "See how he loved him!" But some of them said, "Could not he who opened the eyes of the blind man have kept this man from dying?"

Then Jesus, deeply moved again, came to the tomb; it was a cave, and a stone lay upon it. Jesus said, "Take away the stone." Martha, the sister of the dead man, said to him, "Lord, by this time there will be an odor, for he has been dead four days." Jesus said to her," Did I not tell you that if you would believe you would see the glory of God?" So they took away the stone. And Jesus lifted up his eyes and said, "Father, I thank thee that thou hast heard me. I knew that thou hearest me always, but I have said this on account of the people standing by, that they may believe that thou didst send me." When he had said this, he cried with a loud voice. "Lazarus, come out." The dead man came out, his hands and feet bound with bandages, and his face wrapped with a cloth. Jesus said to them, "Unbind him, and let him go." (John 11:1-4, 17, 32-44)

meditation

In the very midst of life, there is death.

We die many times in this life; and in this life, we witness many deaths around us. We and those we love go through periods of anguish and depression, sickness and suffering, and above all loss – loss of loved ones through physical death and death of relationships, loss of security through crime and unemployment, loss of selfhood by failure and by the relentless numbing fatigue of life. These deaths are as dark and hopeless as the final death that awaits all mortals.

In these periods of death, we are powerless to help ourselves or to help others. We could say that everything is really quite all right, after all: The sun will rise in the morning to the song of the lark, and all will be right with the world. Such an approach trivializes our pain, insults our feelings, and usually gets the sullen look, the sarcastic comment, or the quick insult it deserves.

We could look at our painful death in its cosmic perspective: Just over the horizon people are starving, wars are raging, diseases are rampant. Now we can add to our pain the guilt of being insensitive to the suffering of others. This may even lead us to resent others who suffer – others who are insensitive to our feeling of personal death.

Or we could combat this spiritual death with drugs (either legal or illegal), intoxicants, or self-indulgence. But when we recover from the drug, sober up from the liquor, or put away our newly bought bauble, we find that the death is still there, just as dark and as isolating as ever it had been.

We are like Lazarus in the tomb, alone in the dark, dead, hopeless. Jesus called to Lazarus, and he arose from death. Jesus is calling us as well. Will we arise from death?

When Jesus calls us from our graves, he does not trivialize our pain, for he came down to live the life of a mortal and to suffer painful and humiliating death. He knows the reality of pain. He does not "put us in our place" with guilt, for he considers each one of us to be important by ourselves, not measuring our pain and needs in proportion to the pain and needs of others. He is our personal Savior. Nor does he offer us only a temporary respite, for his great sacrifice – his great "sacred healing deed" – came with no time limit, but lasts for eternity.

To be healers for ourselves and for each other from death in the midst of life, we need to have faith in Christ Jesus. We must pray and trust to establish a right relationship with Christ, and we must do whatever our earthly hands can do as a sign of our commitment to our healing.

Jesus is calling us all from the tomb. We must answer him by doing two things: We must pray and build the trusting relationship of faith with him; and we must help heal one another. This is the Way, as Jesus summed it up in the traditional Hebrew *shema*: "Hear, O Israel: The Lord our God, the Lord is one; and you shall love the Lord your God with all your heart, and with all your soul, and with all your mind, and with all your strength. . . . You shall love your neighbor as yourself" (Mark 12:29b-30, 31b).

In the very midst of death, there is life.

liturgy of prayer

collect

All healing God, who offerest us life in the midst of death, and life eternal in the place of death unending: Assist us in our prayers to build a relationship of healing faith with thee through thy Son our Savior Jesus Christ, and assist us in our works to build a relationship of healing faithfulness with ourselves and with others, that all might be one in Life with thee; through the same Jesus Christ our Lord, who liveth and reigneth with thee and the Holy Spirit, one God, for ever and ever. *Amen.*

hymn: saint beuno

Christ, our healing Lord, redeem us all
from the pains of daily death
that this world in matters great and small
doth inflict with every breath.

Hear us when we pray our souls to thee;
open up our hearts to hear
thine eternal Word, that we might be
ever faithful and sincere.

Let us also give our hearts to those
crying out to us in grief.
Let our love to sufferers disclose
faithfulness and firm belief.

Healing Lord, respond to us we pray:
Heal our hearts, and let us give
loving help to others day by day,
that together we might live.

thanksgiving

We thank thee, Lord, that thou hast given us the example of Saint Beuno to guide us to a more perfect healing in thee.

grace

Almighty and everliving God, by thy Grace let us heal one another and all the world with the spirit of Beuno.

Saint Beuno

Serenely

1. Christ, our heal - ing Lord, re -
2. Hear us when we pray our
3. Let us al - so give our
4. Heal - ing Lord, re - spond to

deem us all from the
souls to thee; o - pen
hearts to those cry - ing
us we pray: Heal our

pains   of   dai -   ly   death
up   our   hearts   to   hear
out   to   us   in   grief.
hearts,   and   let   us   give

that   this   world   in   mat -   ters   great   and
thine   e -   ter -   nal   Word,   that   we   might
Let   our   love   to   suf -   fer -   ers   dis -
lov -   ing   help   to   oth -   ers   day   by

small   doth   in -   flict   with
be   ev -   er   faith -   ful
close   faith -   ful -   ness   and
day,   that   to -   geth -   er

92

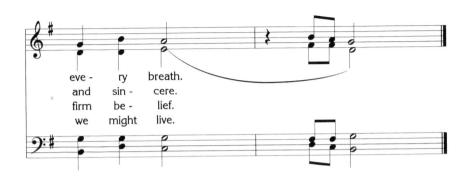

eve - ry breath.
and sin - cere.
firm be - lief.
we might live.

93

Saint Brendan

A Celebration

of Faith

may 16
---
commemoration of saint brendan

saint brendan

Saint Brendan (or Brendon) lived from around 486 to around 575. He founded several monasteries in Ireland and was best known as the abbot of the monastery at Clonfert. He traveled frequently by sea from place to place in the Islands, most likely sailing at least to Scotland (where he reputedly visited Saint Columba in Argyll) and to Wales (where he is said to have served as abbot at Llancarfan).

The use of seaways to connect the monasteries and to spread the Word was a mark of the Celtic Church, and the travels and exploits of "Saint Brendan the Navigator" doubtless represent a collection of legends originally connected with a number of the early saints of Ireland and Britain. We can therefore treat Saint Brendan as the example of the seafaring Celtic Christian who risked his life at the mercy of the chaotic waters to spread and sustain the Gospel in the Western Isles.

The significance of Saint Brendan (together with all the saints he also represents) is indeed profound. Here was a man who spread the Word across the waters just as did God in the very beginning: "And the earth was without form and void, and darkness was upon the face of the deep; and the Spirit of God was moving over the face of the waters" (Genesis 1:2). As God brought his divine order out of the chaos of the waters, so did these brave seafaring monks.

Nor should we forget the personal hardships and the terrors that faced them. The waters threatened from the depths below and the storms above, but they also swarmed with pirates who would show no mercy to the people of God. Surely Saint Brendan was fully aware of the dangers he faced. Yet his love for his God and for his far-flung neighbors was strong enough to compel him to take to the seas, and his faith was strong enough to sustain him through his many trials.

the symbol

Within the circle of the wheel, the three waves of eternity turn, representing the eternal drive of the faithful. This symbol that also stands for the Holy Trinity serves as the sail, fixed securely to a mast that is the cross of Christ. The boat is emblazoned with the Trinity knot, the Three in One – ever connected and never ending. Thus it is that the faith of Saint Brendan is driven over the Chaos of the sea by the Spirit (or Wind) of the Trinity, and yet it is held safely out of the Chaos by the vessel of that same Trinity. Both are connected by the love of Christ – the cross upon which he died for us.

liturgy of the word

holy scripture

One day he got into a boat with his disciples, and he said to them, "Let us go across to the other side of the lake." So they set out, and as they sailed he fell asleep. And a storm of wind came down on the lake, and they were filling with water, and were in danger. And they went and woke him, saying, "Master, Master, we are perishing!" And he awoke and rebuked the wind and the raging waves; and they ceased, and there was a calm. He said to them, "Where is your faith?" And they were afraid, and they marveled, saying to one another, "Who then is this, that he commands even wind and water, and they obey him?" (Luke 8:22-25)

meditation

We are on the boat with Jesus. As he falls asleep in the gently rolling vessel, we are struck by the calmness and serenity that surrounds him and surrounds this little boat on the broad sea. We are at peace.

But the skies darken and the winds start to shriek and whistle around us. A storm comes up and batters our little boat. Quickly the sound of the wind becomes deafening; we cannot stand on the deck; the rain rushes against our faces, taking away our breath and our sight. In our terror we repeat the Breton fisherman's prayer: Preserve me, Lord, for the sea is so wide, and my boat is so small!

Then we remember in our panic: The Son of God is in the boat with us. Rather than calming us down though, knowing he is there makes us more anxious. We scramble across the heaving deck, grasp his arm, and plead for deliverance.

And he looks at us. His eyes see right through our eyes and deep into our very souls with pity, with disappointment, with love. He does not have to ask, "Where is your faith?" He does not have to say anything. We know that we have lacked faith in him, we know that we have failed him, we know that he has already forgiven us.

What is faith? Is it not enough to know that the Son of God is in the very boat with us? Is it not enough to know that he came down to us to share our pain and to allow us to share in his Glory? Is it not enough to know, acknowledge, and believe that He "commands even the wind and water, and they obey him?" No, it is not enough to know these things. We must trust in them.

Faith is being in the boat with Jesus without the slightest concern for the storm that rages around us. As long as Jesus and we are together in the boat – together in this strange and wonderful relationship between "God in man made manifest" and us frail human beings – we are assured that no storm has the power to separate us. In the words of Saint Paul, "For I am sure that neither death, nor life, nor angels, nor principalities, nor things present, nor things to come, nor powers, nor height, nor depth, nor anything else in all creation, will be able to separate us from the love of God in Christ Jesus our Lord" (Romans 8:38-39).

We are on the boat with Jesus. Let us strive to maintain our faith in him that we may not fret over the waves, the wind, and the rain. No wave is so tall, no wind is so strong, no sea is so wide as a boat with Christ Jesus at the helm.

liturgy of prayer

collect

Ever faithful Lord God, who commandest even the winds and water, and they obey thee: Grant us faith that we might never forget that thou art always present with us in our little boat, and that whatever storms and darkness life might inflict upon us, thou shalt ever be with us; through Jesus Christ our Lord, who liveth and reigneth with thee and the Holy Spirit, one God, for ever and ever. *Amen.*

hymn: saint brendan

Upon the wild tempestuous sea,
our little boat is tossed;
and if we put no trust in thee,
our very souls are lost.

In faith let us endure the gale –
no wave can overwhelm,
no wind can tear apart the sail,
when thou art at the helm.

If we but put our trust in thee
that thou wilt keep us sure,
then there is nought upon the sea
that we cannot endure.

Lord, see us through the storms of life
surrounding us each day,
and bring us past this mortal strife
to thine eternal Day.

thanksgiving

We thank thee, Lord, that thou hast given us the example of Saint
Brendan to guide us to a more perfect faith in thee.

grace

Almighty and everliving God, by thy Grace let us hold onto our faith
with the courage and the endurance of Brendan.

Saint Brendan

Resolved

1. U - pon the wild tem -
2. If we but put our

pest - uous sea, our lit - tle boat is
faith in thee that thou wilt keep us

tossed;   and   if   we   put   no
sure,   then   there   is   nought   u -

trust   in   thee,   our   ve -   ry   souls   are
pon   the   sea   that   we   can - not   en -

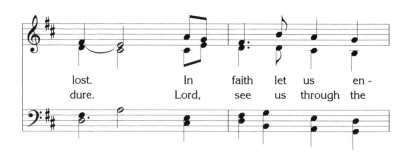

lost.   In   faith   let   us   en -
dure.   Lord,   see   us   through   the

102

dure the gale -- no wave can o - ver -
storms of life sur - round - ing us each

whelm, no wind can tear a -
day, and bring us past this

part the sail, when thou art at the helm.
mor - tal strife to thine e -ter - nal Day.

Saint Columba

A Celebration
of Harmony

june 9
---
commemoration of saint columba

saint columba

Saint Columba (or Colum-cille in the Gaelic) was a giant in the Celtic monastic movement. Monasteries in the Celtic Church were not the isolated islands of tranquility in a troubled secular sea that they are often seen as today. Rather, they were the headquarters and refuges of Christianity. The abbot often had more power than the bishop, and the monastery functioned as a Christian community from which monks would be dispatched to serve the surrounding area and to which they would return for renewal and education. In times of invasion, these monasteries would also be the strongholds to which the laity – the people of God – would flee for safety.

Saint Columba left his native Ireland to go to Scotland, which was then an Irish colony carved out of the Pictish lands north of the Britons. There are several different versions as to why he left Ireland and how many monasteries he established in Scotland. One overriding and certain fact remains, however: On the twelfth day of May in the year 563 he founded the Community of Iona, one of the most influential of such establishments in the Christian world.

The mark of Saint Columba's ministry was harmonious community. He brought into Iona believers from all over the British Isles and Europe. Included in this community were even believers from the then predominantly pagan Angles and Saxons. These Germanic invaders were viewed by most Celtic Christians as enemies so feared and despised that the Church was hard-pressed to find missionaries who would even approach them. And his drive for inclusion also led him to the north, where he converted Brude, a king of the Picts.

His relations with Ireland flourished, and he found himself put further to the test as a community builder in his negotiations between the Gaels in Scotland and those in the Irish homeland. As a supervisor of monasteries in Ireland and in the colonies, he avoided the rifts that arose all too easily in communities separated by often hostile waters, and he sustained the harmony of the Gaelic Church.

Moreover, his community was not to be simply a collection of theologians. He supported the institution of the bard – of which he himself was a member – and ensured that it would flourish not as an entity apart from the Church, but as an integral part of it, marrying song with Scripture, lore with Tradition, laity with clergy. Reaching out to the traditions of the Celts, he declared "My Druid is Christ," a brave comparison indeed in a Church that often viewed druidism as necessarily pagan and that just as often set as its goal the eradication of all pre-Christian institutions. Saint Columba, however, saw harmony between the cultural tradition and the Scriptures and recognized that all learning had value and could be used for the good of the Church.

In everything he did, Saint Columba honored the words of Saint Paul: "Welcome one another, therefore, as Christ has welcomed you, for the glory of God" (Romans 15:7)

the symbol

At the far ends of the cross, interwoven Trinity knots represent communities of the people of God, who traditionally bestows on each a three-fold measure of his Grace. But no community by itself can prosper, for it will soon look only inward and forget that it is a part of the greater Body of Christ. Thus, the communities must be joined to one another through the Wisdom knot in the heart of the cross – the loving Sophia of Christ. This is the harmony among many diverse Christian communities that Saint Columba achieved in Iona. Moreover, as the wheel of humanity spans from community to community outside the cross, we are reminded of the need to spread the Word to all those who live in the void between communities and to bring them within the cross of our Lord.

liturgy of the word

holy scripture

Therefore encourage one another and build one another up, just as you are doing.

But we beseech you, brethren, to respect those who labor among you and are over you in the Lord and admonish you, and to esteem them very highly in love because of their work. Be at peace among yourselves. And we exhort you, brethren, admonish the idle, encourage the faint-hearted, help the weak, be patient with them all. See that none of you repays evil for evil, but always seek to do good to one another and to all. Rejoice always, pray constantly, give thanks in all circumstances; for this is the will of God in Christ Jesus for you. Do not quench the Spirit, do not despise prophesying, but test everything; hold fast what is good, abstain from every form of evil.

May the God of peace himself sanctify you wholly; and may your spirit and soul and body be kept sound and blameless at the coming of our Lord Jesus Christ. He who calls you is faithful, and he will do it.

Brethren, pray for us.

Greet all the brethren with a holy kiss.

(1 Thessalonians 5:11-26)

medítatíon

We kneel at our pew in church, fervently praying to God for his Steadfast Love and for the forgiveness of our many sins – of what we have done and of what we have left undone. We close our eyes to shut out all distractions, and we feel ourselves in perfect and special communion with God. In our darkness and isolation, we do not see the world around us; and in our devout concentration, we do not hear the prayers of the others in church.

It strikes us that this is an ideal world. We are at one with God, and God fills us with his holy and healing peace. We are as an only child basking in the loving care of the holy Parent. Nothing could disturb our serenity; nothing could jar our certainty; nothing could remove us from this feeling of loving communion.

Then we open our eyes. Before us we see a brother in Christ who sold us some property. We knew that the property contained a rich vein of gold, but he did not know this. We consider ourselves wise in achieving a great profit.

Before us we see a sister in Christ who applied for a position where we work. We were afraid that her credentials looked far better than ours and that she would surpass us in a short time. So we found fault with her work, claiming that some small oversight of hers in her résumé was a calamity that reflected major incompetence. She did not get the position. We consider ourselves wise in maintaining our security.

And we see many other brethren. Some disagreed with us on church matters, and we managed to convince the congregation that they were not truly Christian. Others have different ethnic backgrounds, and we convinced our church groups that they "did not fit." We consider ourselves wise in our politics.

We are smug in our position of power and authority over our brethren, until we realize that now we do not feel the same loving communion with God that we felt while we prayed with our eyes closed to those around us. Do we close our eyes again and ask once more for God's Steadfast Love and his eternal forgiveness? Or do we face our brethren, ask them for their love and forgiveness, join with them arm in arm and pray together, lifting our voices as one in the communal harmony of praise and thanksgiving?

liturgy of prayer

collect

Great God and Lord of all, who lovest us all and individually in our community: Teach us we pray to share with one another in perfect harmony that same Steadfast Love that thou hast shown to us in the death of thine only begotten Son Jesus Christ for our sake, that we might raise our voices together in praise and thanksgiving to thee; through the same Jesus Christ our Lord, who liveth and reigneth with thee and the Holy Spirit, one God, for ever and ever. *Amen.*

hymn: saint columba

Thou art the Maker of us all
and givest all thy Steadfast Love,
that we might ever on thee call
with prayers below to thee above.

Let me not shut mine eyes to thee
nor to my neighbor, whom thou too
dost love just as thou lovest me –
divinely steadfast, good, and true.

Let us our differences reject –
our gain at one another's loss –
and with one voice in joy elect
the better way, the loving Cross.

We stand together arm in arm
to pray to God in harmony;
we pledge to do no earthly harm
to those we share in love with thee.

thanksgiving

We thank thee, Lord, that thou hast given us the example of Saint Columba to guide us to a more perfect community in thee.

grace

Almighty and everliving God, by thy Grace let live with one another in harmony, as Columba hath shown us.

Saint Columba

Solidly

1. Thou art the mak - er
2. Let me not shut mine
3. Let us our dif - ferenc -
4. We stand to - geth - er

of us all and giv - est all thy
eyes to thee nor to my neigh - bor,
es re - ject -- our gain at one an -
arm in arm to pray to God in

Stead - fast Love, that we might ev - er
whom thou too dost love just as thou
oth - er's loss -- and with one voice in
har - mo - ny; we pledge to do no

on thee call with prayers be - low to
lov - est me -- di - vine - ly stead - fast,
joy e - lect the bet - ter way, the
earth - ly harm to those we share in

thee a - bove.
good, and true.
lov - ing Cross.
love with thee.

113

Saint Monenna

A Celebration
of Humility

july 6
---
commemoration of
saint monenna

saint monenna

Today many people are familiar with the two patron saints of
Ireland: Patrick of Armagh and Brigid of Kildare. Saint Patrick helped
spread the Word from Britain to Ireland, and Saint Brigid gave it her
love, care, and compassion and kept the fire of the Holy Spirit
burning. Yet, in their shadow another saint quietly worked her way
into the hearts of God's people. This was Saint Monenna (also known
as Darerca or Bline), who died around the year 518.

She is well beloved, and her feast day is still observed; and yet, so
very little is known about her. What we do know, however, makes this
situation seem altogether fitting. For although she would dearly value
our love, she would certainly shrink from our attention.

Saint Monenna founded a nunnery with eight virgins and one
widow. They lived in extreme poverty, giving rather to the poor all the
food and clothing beyond that which they needed to subsist. At a time
when the saints were often connected with royal families and well
before the calls to poverty of such saints as Francis and Clare of
Assisi, Monenna chose the path of humility, serving God by being a
servant to his people.

At the nunnery, the son of the widow was nurtured in the Word
and went on to become a bishop. One of the virgins was sent to Saint
Ninian to learn and flourish in the Spirit and to bring the model of
Whithorn back to her sisters. Saint Monenna herself, however,
remained back in Killeevy in quiet, in poverty, and in humility building
her little nunnery into a prominent abbey.

116

the symbol

Humility within the cross of Christ has three characteristics that are represented in the symbol for Saint Monenna. Firstly, we are all as one within the Body of Christ; thus, the area within the cross is solid, with no turning paths and no divisions that could separate a person in one part of the cross from a person in another part. Secondly, we are all equal within the love of Christ; thus, the arms of the cross are equal, so that no one arm – no one Christian – is closer or further from the heart of the cross. Thirdly, we are all equal in relationship with one another; thus, the cross is unadorned, so that no one part might be judged more important or illustrious than any other part.

liturgy of the word

holy scripture

Then the mother of the sons of Zebedee came up to him, with her sons, and kneeling before him she asked him for something. And he said to her, "What do you want?" She said to him, "Command that these two sons of mine may sit, one at your right hand and one at your left, in your kingdom."

117

But Jesus answered, "You do no know what you are asking. Are you able to drink the cup that I am to drink?" They said to him, "We are able." He said to them, "You will drink my cup, but to sit at my right hand and at my left is not mine to grant, but it is for those for whom it has been prepared by my Father." And when the ten heard it, they were indignant at the two brothers. But Jesus called them to him and said, "You know that the rulers of the Gentiles exercise authority over them. It shall not be so among you; but whoever would be great among you must be your servant, and whoever would be first among you must be your slave; even as the Son of man came not to be served but to serve, and to give his life as a ransom for many." (Matthew 20:20-28)

meditation

We feel very uncomfortable about the concept of Christian humility and equality. Like the Gentiles Christ alludes to, we seem to be of the opinion that those who do the most prominent work should be exalted over the rest. After all, this is the way we run our professional and social lives – the boss sits above the workers, the first family of the community sits above the other citizens.

How would we really feel if the boss came down into our midst and said that he or she was there to help us do our jobs and to please let him or her know what needs to be done? First, we would probably not believe it, but would wait for the boss to put aside the charade and reveal the real message for the day. Of course, we would not want to say anything, fearing a trick that would identify us as disgruntled employees. No matter how genuine the boss' intent, we would never feel comfortable all on the same level. Indeed, nothing – not even the power to fire the boss – would ever overcome our suspicions.

118

Jesus constantly reminds us of our equality in humility – that no one sits higher than anyone else. Even God through his Son placed himself on our level; and when God had become flesh to suffer with us in our humility and even to die as a mortal, he manifested himself not as a mighty tyrant, but as a servant. He went so far as to wash his disciples' feet – the job of the lowliest servant of a household.

Indeed, it used to be that we addressed the Holy Trinity not with the form of respect, but with the form of familiarity. The word *thou* in English was once used only with one's most intimate friends, with one's immediate family, and with and among children. Now, it is never heard outside of prayer, where it is often misperceived as a special form of respect. We simply could not stand to have God on our level and intimately connected with us.

In the church, the ministers used to be those members of God's people (all known as the "laity") who served the rest. They would stand in the midst of the congregation and on the same level or even lower. Now, we elevate the minister and separate him or her from the congregation (whom we often think of as "only the laity"). We consider the "minister" not to be the person who serves us, but the person we obey; and we consider the act of "ministering" to involve not the care of our needs, but the exercise of authority.

The word "humility" comes from the word "humus." In it, we recognize that we all come from the same clay, and we shall all return to that same clay. By what right does one piece of clay place itself over another; and by what reason does one piece of clay submit itself to another? To act in humility is to treat others "on ground level" – as equals in Christ.

liturgy of prayer

collect

All encompassing God, who didst come to dwell amongst us, to take on our form of clay, to suffer pain and death as one of us, and thereby to show us thy Way of humility: Grant that we may overcome the perverse spirit that seeks to place one above another and replace it with the true Spirit, so that as thou dost dwell as Creator, Redeemer, and Sustainer all in one and in equal substance, so might we too dwell with one another in equal substance; through Jesus Christ our Lord, who liveth and reigneth with thee and the Holy Spirit, one God, for ever and ever. *Amen.*

hymn: saint monenna

Lord, teach us to live in humility,
to love all of those with whom we toil,
to deal with each other in equality,
remembering we come from the soil.

Let pride not seduce, nor power corrupt,
nor envy our harmony destroy;
and let us not fight lest our anger erupt,
but let us humility employ.

Lord, show us that we are one in thy sight,
that each child is precious in thy heart,
that strength doth not alter a wrong to a right,
nor rank special privileges impart.

In humility, let us live as one,
ignoring what differences could
make us see another as someone to shun,
but let us see one another's good.

thanksgiving

We thank thee, Lord, that thou hast given us the example of Saint Monenna to guide us to a more perfect humility in thee.

grace

Almighty and everliving God, by thy Grace let us be content to live humbly in harmony with thee and with one another as did Monenna.

Saint Monenna

Solidly

1. Lord, teach us to live in hu - mil - i -
2. Let pride not se - duce nor pow - er cor -
3. Lord, show us that we are one in thy
4. In hu - mil - i - ty, let us live as

ty,   to   love   all   of
rupt,   nor   en -   vy   our
sight,   that each   child is
one,   ig - nor - ing   what

those   with whom   we
har -   mon - y   de -
prec -   ious in   thy
dif -   fer - enc - es

toil,   to   deal   with each
stroy;   and   let   us   not
heart,   that strength doth not
could   make us   see   an -

123

Saint Samson

A Celebration
of Mission

july 28
---
commemoration of
saint samson

saint samson

Together with Saints David and Hildutus, Saint Samson is one of the three major saints of Wales consecrated by Saint Dubricius. This sixth-century bishop occupies a position in the British Church that typifies his most salient characteristic – mission. As Dubricius passed on the loving burden of the church to David as the keeper of the flock and to Hildutus as the keeper of learning, so he passed on to Samson the responsibility of keeping the church united within the greater body of Christ and of bringing ever more people into it.

His mission, however, did not come immediately to him. As a child, he was sent to Saint Hildutus to become educated in Scripture and in philosophy. From there, he became a cellarer on Caldey Island (Ynys Byr), seeking solitude for quiet reflection. But this was not to be, for he was soon thrust into the responsibility of being an abbot, taking charge of his monks and ensuring the peace of his district. His ability was noted in Ireland, and he was called to a monastery there.

After he reformed this monastery, he tried once again to lead the solitary life of a hermit along the banks of the Severn. And once again, he was called to be abbot of a nearby monastery. Now it became obvious to him that God was not calling him to a life of quiet reflection, but to a life of active mission. Giving his life into God's hands, he embarked upon one of the most remarkably energetic and influential missionary careers in the history of the Church.

His first mission in his new calling was across the Severn in Cornwall, where he established churches and monasteries. From there, he traveled all around the Isles bringing the Word by showing the Word. While church dedications abound for all the major saints, Saint Samson's far-flung flock named an entire island in Scilly after him.

Finally, he moved across the Channel to Brittany, founding monasteries from Dol in Brittany all the way to Pental in Normandy. In Dol, he took up the crozier of bishop and exercised responsibility over the administration of a large ecclesiastical area (at the time involving civil and judicial duties as well), and from this base he spread the Word far and wide. He was most probably the Bishop Samson who signed the acts of the Council of Paris in 557.

Nor did his mission end there. His name was so revered not only among the Celts, but even among the newly converted Saxons that six churches were dedicated to him in Saxon England; and centuries after the saint's death, King Athelstan of Wessex obtained the saint's crozier for a monastery in Dorset.

Not even death could hold Saint Samson from his mission.

the symbol

Centered within the cross of Christ Jesus is a knot similar to Saint Patrick's interlocking Trinity knots, but there are four points. These represent the four points of the compass, to which Saint Samson went on his life of mission for his God. These points connect the center – the heart of the cross – with all of God's people out on the rim of the wheel, just as it is through their dedication to mission that the saints join the love of Christ with all of humanity. Just as with Saint Patrick's interlocking knots, where the knots of mission connect with one another, hearts form to convey the Steadfast Love of God from the center of the cross – the symbol of suffering and triumphant love – to all people, no matter in what direction they may live. And it

127

is through the mission of the saints that we are all interconnected with the Cross of our Lord and Savior.

liturgy of the word

holy scripture

O sing to the LORD a new song;
    sing to the LORD, all the earth!
Sing to the LORD, bless his name;
    tell of his salvation from day to day.
Declare his glory among the nations,
    his marvelous works among all the peoples!
For great is the LORD, and greatly to be praised;
    he is to be feared above all gods.
For all the gods of the peoples are idols;
    but the LORD made the heavens.
Honor and majesty are before him;
    strength and beauty are in his sanctuary.
Ascribe to the LORD, O families of the peoples,
    ascribe to the LORD glory and strength!
Ascribe to the LORD the glory due his name;
    bring an offering, and come into his courts!
Worship the LORD in holy array;
    tremble before him, all the earth!

Say among the nations, "The LORD reigns!
    Yea, the world is established, it shall never be moved;
he will judge the peoples with equity."

Let the heavens be glad, and let the earth rejoice;
     let the sea roar, and all that fills it;
     let the field exult, and everything in it!
Then shall all the trees of the wood sing for joy
     before the LORD, for he comes,
     for he comes to judge the earth.
He will judge the world with righteousness,
     and the peoples with his truth. (Psalm 96)

And Jesus came and said to them "All authority in
heaven and on earth has been given to me. Go
therefore and make disciples of all nations, baptizing
them in the name of the Father and of the Son and
of the Holy Spirit, teaching them to observe all that
I have commanded you; and lo, I am with you
always, to the close of the age." (Matthew 28:18-20)

meditation

Do we have a mission? Those who work in large organizations –
from the military to the corporation, from the university to the church
– dread this question. It means forming committees and wasting time
to come up with a statement that sounds important. Once the
mission statement is adopted, it is reproduced in endless documents
and fundamentally ignored.

But do we *have a mission*? By this we mean not some mission
statement drawn up to justify our position within an organization, but
an actual mission – a calling to perform a genuine service to God and
humanity. Do we have a *mission*?

This is an even more dreaded question, for we must answer it not
to justify ourselves to others, but to justify ourselves to us. This
requires a judgement, measuring ourselves against an ideal and
seeing how well we live up to the ideals we profess. And as with all

129

self-judgements – from those we make about ourselves every day to the Final Judgement before our eyes and the eyes of the Lord – we are facing self-doubt and fear.

We know that we have a mission. We know that the mission comes to us from God through Christ Jesus and with the support of the Holy Spirit. We have read the Scriptures, and perhaps we have even heard a calling within us. So we know what the mission is. Yet, we daily silence that still small voice calling within us and "postpone" the mission, choosing to justify ourselves rather by excuses than by deeds.

We choose to use the talents God has given us not to further his Kingdom on earth, but to enhance our standing among others. In effect, we are treating our holy mission as though it were our corporate mission statement. We devise important and religious sounding phrases to make it appear as though we are performing this mission, while all we are doing is marking time while we pursue our own ambitions. We have turned the divine mission into the mundane mission statement.

When we receive a call to mission, it is natural to question it. Even Moses questioned his mission to lead his people out of Egypt. Many people have embarked on missions that have failed or that have even made matters worse. But that is no excuse for us. Is it not better to answer a call and fail than to succeed in ignoring a call from God? We know the answer. We have our excuses ready. How long can we resist?

The best excuse is this: How do we know just exactly what our particular mission is? To find this out, we must do something that we also avoid by whatever pressing excuses we can find. We must retreat into a quiet room and sit – sit not until we are tired of sitting and think of something that must be done right away, but sit until God's will begins to be revealed.

Our mission will not come to us in our first sitting, and the first revelations are most likely to be: Wait, but continue to pray. If we continue this quiet but expectant prayer regimen, we will eventually receive our revelation, our mission. It will come when God knows we are ready; but we can only be ready if we open ourselves to his will by contemplative and receptive prayer.

liturgy of prayer

collect

Lord God, who hearest our prayers gladly but who wilt that we should pray more to hear thee: Open our inner ears that we might hear the mission that thou wouldst have us embark upon, open our minds that we might receive thy divine revelation through the Way of thine only true and adorable Son, and open our hearts that we might be sustained by the Holy Spirit in thy steadfast service; through the same Jesus Christ our Lord, who liveth and reigneth with thee and the Holy Spirit, one God, for ever and ever. *Amen.*

hymn: saint samson

Lord, send us out to spread thy Word
despite the doubt that would delay
our mission for our gracious Lord
who careth for us on our way.

How often we refuse to hear
the whispered plea that thou dost give,
objecting to thy message clear
as creatures who "have lives to live."

But is it not our rule of life,
which we forgot in comfort's sloth,
that we proclaim despite all strife
thy holy Name, our sacred troth?

131

Lord, stir our blood, command that we
confront the flood of base desire
that drowneth will in lethargy.
Oh Lord, instill in us thy fire.

thanksgiving

We thank thee, Lord, that thou hast given us the example of Saint
Samson to guide us to a more perfect mission in thee.

grace

Almighty and everliving God, by thy Grace let us dedicate ourselves
to the mission thou hast prepared for us with the determination of
Samson.

Saint Samson

would de - lay our mis - sion for our
thou dost give, ob - ject - ing to thy
com - fort's sloth, that we pro- claim de -
base de - sire that drown - eth will in

grac - ious Lord who car - eth for us
mes - sage clear as crea - tures who "have
spite all strife thy ho - ly Name, our
leth - ar - gy. Oh Lord, in - still in

on our way.
lives to live."
sa - cred troth?
us thy fire.

Saint Ninian

A Celebration
of Bravery

august 26
---
commemoration of
saint ninian

saint ninian

Saint Ninian (or Nynia) lived in the fifth century, at the very beginning of the Dark Ages in Britain. Most of our information on him comes to us from the Venerable Bede, and for a long time Bede's account was doubted regarding this saint, where he ministered, and what he did. Recent archaeological evidence, however, rather supports both the accuracy of our historian and the works of our saint.

To understand the importance of Saint Ninian in the Celtic Church of the Dark Ages, we must first look at some background. He was known as the apostle to the Picts, who were so called because they painted themselves (Latin *picti* 'the painted ones') in a warrior pagan tradition that had long since died out among the Britons to the south. These Picts lived beyond the limits of the Roman Empire, where Hadrian's Wall was erected to keep them out. But the last Roman troops withdrew from Britain in 410, leaving the protection of the south in the hands of small, feuding, disorganized realms. Soon the Picts were pressing southward. In 449, the Saxons and other Germanic tribes established a permanent foothold in Britain and launched raids around the coasts. Meanwhile, Gaelic pirates were also raiding the western coastal regions and were launching their own invasions of Pictland and northern Britain, which would later become Scotland.

In the very thick of this chaos, Saint Ninian established a monastery at Whithorn, which he called *Candida Casa* 'White House'.

In faithfulness to God and in defiance of all around him, he stood firmly within the tradition of Joshua: "And if you be unwilling to serve the LORD, choose this day whom you will serve, whether the gods your fathers served in the region beyond the River, or the gods of the Amorites in whose land you dwell; but as for me and my house, we will serve the LORD" (Joshua 24:15).

At *Candida Casa* his bravery for the Lord was put to the test. As apostle to the Picts, he worked to convert these same people who were pressing their invasions of Britain. In maintaining his position on the coast where he could take advantage of the dangerous sea routes to spread the Word, he laid himself open to attacks from Gaelic pirates, Irish/Scottish invaders, and Saxon raiders. But Saint Ninian held firm, braved the dangerous roads and seaways, and established a number of churches in Pictland and in the realms of the northern Britons.

the symbol

The bravery of Saint Ninian is represented by a shield without a sword. This is a frightening image for us humans – one that indeed shows great bravery: No matter how pressing the attacks fall upon us, we cannot fight back. How, then, can we succeed if we can do nothing but shield ourselves? The answer is found within the symbol, in which we see that the shield flows from the power of the Holy Trinity and is interwoven with the cross of the all-conquering love of Christ Jesus. Our shield is both behind the cross and in front of it, for the love of Christ preserves us as we must preserve the beloved church – not by fighting the people of God, but ever by defending them.

liturgy of the word

holy scripture

When Daniel knew that the document had been signed, he went to his home where he had windows in his upper chamber open toward Jerusalem; and he got down upon his knees three times a day and prayed and gave thanks before his God, as he had done previously. Then these men came by agreement and found Daniel making petition and supplication before his God. Then they came near and said before the king, concerning the interdict, "O king! Did you not sign an interdict, that any man who makes petition to any god or man within thirty days except to you, O king, shall be cast into the den of lions?" The king answered, "The thing stands fast, according to the law of the Medes and Persians, which cannot be revoked." Then they answered before the king, "That Daniel who is one of the exiles from Judah, pays no heed to you, O king, or the interdict you have signed, but makes his petition three times a day."

Then the king, when he heard these words, was much distressed, and set his mind to deliver Daniel; and he labored till the sun went down to rescue him. Then these men came by agreement to the king, and said to the king, "Know, O king , that it is a law of the Medes and Persians that no interdict or ordinance which the king establishes can be changed."

Then the king commanded, and Daniel was brought and cast into the den of lions. The king said to Daniel, "May your God, whom you serve continually, deliver you!" And a stone was brought and laid upon the mouth of the den, and the king sealed it with his own signet and with the signet of his lords, that nothing might be changed concerning Daniel. Then the king went to his palace, and spent the night fasting; no diversions were brought to him, and sleep fled from him.

Then, at the break of day, the king arose and went in haste to the den of lions. When he came near to the den where Daniel was, he cried out in a tone of anguish and said to Daniel, "O Daniel, servant of the living God, has your God, whom you serve continually, been able to deliver you from the lions?" Then Daniel said to the king, "O king, live for ever! My God sent his angel and shut the lions' mouths, and they have not hurt me, because I was found blameless before him; and also before you, O king, I have done no wrong." Then the king was exceedingly glad, and commanded that Daniel be taken up out of the den. So Daniel was taken up out of the den, and no kind of hurt was found upon him, because he had trusted in his God. (Daniel 6:10-23)

meditation

There are times when we feel that the whole world is collapsing in upon us. All our best efforts have resulted in miserable failure. Everywhere we turn, we see adversity and adversaries, as though we were with Daniel in the den of lions. Our friends, whom we have helped so often in the past and upon whom we find ourselves now relying so greatly for help, suddenly all vanish into the mist, leaving us alone. We desperately need at least to hear from members of our family for just a word of encouragement, but they are silent.

At times like these, we are like the last outpost of a Roman Empire that has been chipped away from without and washed away from within. We stand alone and forlorn behind crumbling walls. And somewhere "out there" we can feel our fate closing in on us. We cannot run; we cannot surrender; and we most assuredly know we cannot win. We stand alone on a hill, feeling the wind of fate blow around us.

What can we do when we know we must do something and yet we know there is nothing we can do for ourselves?

This is the point of most joyous freedom. We are free from ourselves, for we know there is nothing left for us to do for ourselves. Now is the time to turn to God in prayer and ask not that he save us by some divine miracle, but that he tell us what we can do for him. Now is the time to pray for bravery in the service of the Lord our God.

If we are alone and surrounded by enemies, if we are cast into a den of lions, there is no amount of bravery that will save us. So let us toss off this concern for our own lives, and let us pray to find a way to serve God in the midst of utter adversity. Then, if we fall into failure or death for ourselves, we might still provide an example of steadfast loyalty to God. But if by some miracle we attain success and life, we will know that it is not through some selfish, self-centered interest that we are saved, but for the greater Glory of our Lord and Savior.

Whether we succeed or whether we fail in our earthly struggles, in the very end we all come to nought. If our personal success is all that we have lived for, there will have been no life. Success comes only through him who said: "For whoever would save his life will lose it; and whoever loses his life for my sake, he will save it" (Luke 9:24).

liturgy of prayer

collect

Ever victorious God, who hast promised Light and Life to all who shall seek them through thee: Grant us the wisdom in times of adversity to know that our salvation cometh only through thee and the courage to act bravely for thy sake and for the sake and Glory of our Lord and Savior Jesus Christ; through the same Jesus Christ our Lord, who liveth and reigneth with thee and the Holy Spirit, one God, for ever and ever. *Amen.*

hymn: saint ninian

When the arrows fall all around our head
and we hear the trumpets of doom,
we lift up our eyes and ignore the dread
and remember our Christ's dark tomb,

where he lay in bondage to death for us,
so that we no longer might die;
and he rose from that dread sarcophagus
to live on in Heaven on high.

Let us lift our heads and proclaim our Lord
in the face of failure and loss;
and with courage in the almighty Word
let us bravely lift up our cross.

141

For there is no death that can end our Life,
if we live in Christ and obey
his eternal Word through the midst of strife
and we follow him in his Way.

thanksgiving

We thank thee, Lord, that thou hast given us the example of Saint Ninian to guide us to a more perfect bravery in thee.

grace

Almighty and everliving God, by thy Grace let us remain as bravely steadfast as Ninian through all adversity.

Saint Ninian

Slow March

1. When the ar - rows fall all a -
2. where he lay in bond - age to
3. Let us lift our heads and pro -
4. For there is no death that can

round our head and we hear the trum - pets of
death for us. so that we no long - er might
claim our Lord in the face of fail - ure and
end our Life, if we live in Christ and o -

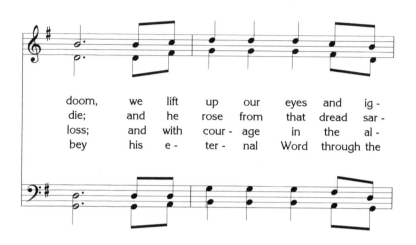

doom,	we	lift	up	our	eyes	and	ig -
die;	and	he	rose	from	that	dread	sar -
loss;	and	with	cour -	age	in	the	al -
bey	his	e -	ter -	nal	Word	through the

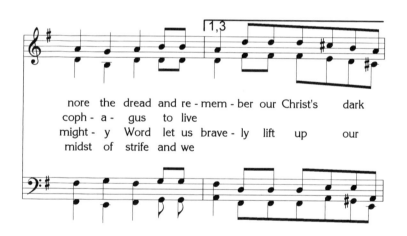

nore	the	dread	and	re -	mem -	ber	our	Christ's	dark
coph -	a -	gus	to	live
might -	y	Word	let	us	brave -	ly	lift	up	our
midst	of	strife	and	we

144

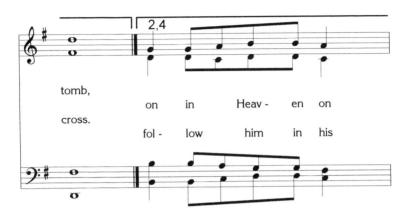

tomb,

cross.

on   in   Heav -   en   on

fol -   low   him   in   his

high.

Way.

Saint Ciaran

A Celebration

of Grace

september 9
---
commemoration of saint ciaran

saint ciaran

Saint Ciaran (also Ceran, Kieran, Queran) of Clonmacnois was one of the most Christ-like of the Irish saints, and his short life is for us both sad and uplifting. Like Jesus, he was born into poverty. While other saints were sons and daughters of prominent Celtic leaders, Ciaran's father was an itinerant carpenter, not unlike Saint Joseph. Ciaran was born around the year 512.

His family was too humble to arrange for his education through foster parents or through a donation to a monastery, but they could give him a cow to take with him to Saint Finnian of Clonnard. Saint Ciaran studied intensely at Clonnard supposedly with only the nourishment afforded by this single cow's milk. As a monk, he traveled to Saint Enda on the Island of Aran, where he was ordained a priest about the year 534. He went on to serve under Saint Senan on Scattery Island around 541.

Late in 544, he journeyed to Clonmacnois and established what would become one of the largest and most important monasteries in Ireland, a center of learning and a bulwark of the Faith throughout the hard times to come. But Saint Ciaran saw nothing of its greatness, for within a year he died, probably trying to save his flock from the yellow plague that swept through the Celtic lands. Like Jesus, he was only thirty-three when he breathed his last earthly sigh.

The sad part of Saint Ciaran's life was the ungraciousness with which he was treated by other clergy. There were those who were jealous of Ciaran's goodness, his success in learning, and in his

148

unswerving friendship to others. They saw that his qualities justly reflected his close relationship with God, and they could not understand how one so lowly could be so obviously beloved by their Lord. Like the older brothers of Joseph, they envied his closeness to the Father, and it is said that all the saints of Ireland save Saint Columba prayed for his early demise.

The uplifting part of Saint Ciaran's life was the graciousness with which he treated those who envied and despised him. From an humble peasant girl whom he directed to become a nun to the imposing King Diarmait of Ireland whom he counseled, Ciaran offered himself as friend and confidant, showing no favor by riches or power, but only the charity of Christian humility.

In a vision he shared with Saint Enda on Aran, a magnificent and fruitful tree spread over all of Ireland. Birds came from around the world to share in the fruit of that tree. Enda identified the tree as Ciaran himself, covering and protecting Ireland with his grace, and spreading this grace to all through his acts of piety and charity.

the symbol

In the center of the symbol for Saint Ciaran is the Trinity knot, for Grace flows from God to us through the Holy Trinity. The grace that we show to each other flows from this Grace, as do the smaller Trinity knots on the wheel of humanity. These acts of grace connect us all not only with God, but also with each other in a never-ending flow of grace. The flow of grace through humanity is also intertwined with the cross of Christ, for in giving his only begotten Son that we might Live, God has offered us the most perfect Grace. And in showing one another grace, we demonstrate that we are bound up in this Grace and in the love of Jesus Christ our Lord.

liturgy of the word

holy scripture

May grace and peace be multiplied to you in the knowledge of God and of Jesus our Lord.

His divine power has granted to us all things that pertain to life and godliness, through the knowledge of him who called us to his own glory and excellence, by which he has granted to us his precious and very great promises, that through these you may escape from the corruption that is in the world because of passion, and become partakers of the divine nature. For this very reason make every effort to supplement your faith with virtue, and virtue with knowledge, and knowledge with self-control, and self-control with steadfastness, and steadfastness with godliness, and godliness with brotherly affection, and brotherly affection with love. For if these things are yours and abound, they keep you from being ineffective or unfruitful in the knowledge of our Lord Jesus Christ. (2 Peter 1:2-8)

meditation

There will always be those who envy us for whatever reason and who wish us ill. Knowing ourselves, our motivations, and our limitations differently than they do, we may well be mystified as to why they should be jealous of us. Nonetheless, we are painfully aware of their ill-will.

When this happens, we often draw ourselves back behind our spiritual fortifications and see to our defense. We are besieged, and we feel it necessary to oppose those who oppose us. Moreover, we are wrongfully besieged, and indignation rises up to bolster our determined defense.

The more unreasonable the ill-will of our opponents seems to us, the more irrational they appear. The more irrational they become in our view, the less human and the less Christian they appear. As their humanity and Christianity plummet before our eyes, the more justified we become in naming them opponents, enemies, servants of the anti-Christ. Whatever ill-will they direct at us, we are fully – even religiously – justified in throwing back twenty-fold at them.

This is vengeance. To be sure, it is not the vengeance that spills blood and leads to generations of feuding; but it is vengeance nevertheless, for in our spirits we are giving back measure-for-measure the ill-will of our opponents. And of course, it is we who consider what measure of our enmity equals a measure of the enmity "wrongfully" directed against us ("wrongfully," that is, until our opponents perceive our ill-will, thus justifying their envy and suspicion).

How do we stop this spiritual feud and return to the love and fellowship commanded of us by our Lord Jesus Christ? Above all, we need two elements: knowledge and grace. First, we must seek to know why these people wish us ill. It is up to us to find out, not up to them to come to us. As Jesus said, "So if you are offering your gift at the altar, and there remember that your brother has something against you, leave your gift there before the altar and go; first be reconciled to your brother, and then come and offer your gift" (Matthew 5:23-24).

The other element is grace. We have our whole lives long transgressed against God, and we continue to transgress to such a degree that it is only through his Grace manifest in Christ Jesus that we are reconciled to him. When people wish us ill, it is up to us to extend our grace to them and to keep extending it for as long as God extends his Grace to us.

Through seeking to know others and to give them our grace, we act as peacemakers, and thus, by doing the will of our Father in heaven, we become his children. When he said, "Blessed are the peacemakers, for they shall be called sons of God" (Matthew 5:9), Jesus was offering consolation to those who take on this difficult and truly thankless task, for those who dwell in the comfort of their envy seldom appreciate overtures of peace. Yet, if we are to be the children of God, we must overcome envy with grace.

liturgy of prayer

collect

Almighty and gracious God, who hast promised us Grace and life eternal in the Word of Christ Jesus our Lord: Strengthen us in the determination to pass on thy perfect Grace through our own humble grace to others, especially to those who envy us and wish us ill, that through our grace all may see the glory of thine; through the same Jesus Christ our Lord, who liveth and reigneth with thee and the Holy Spirit, one God, for ever and ever. *Amen.*

hymn: saint ciaran

The Grace of God surpasseth all mortal understanding.
With reason clouded by the Fall, we are at a loss
to comprehend his Steadfast Love, graciously commanding
we love each other, as above he doth from the Cross.

Though people envy us and wish ill upon us often
and view our acts as devilish when we try for good,
let us be gracious to them all, hard hearts let us soften,
and seek our neighbors to recall to our brotherhood.

thanksgiving

We thank thee, Lord, that thou hast given us the example of Saint
Ciaran to guide us to a more perfect grace in thee.

grace

Almighty and everliving God, by thy Grace let us treat one another
with the generosity and the grace of Ciaran.

Saint Ciaran

Flowing

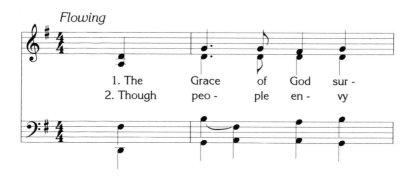

1. The Grace of God sur -
2. Though peo - ple en - vy

pass- eth all mor - tal un - der -
us and wish ill u - pon us

stand - ing.   With   rea - son   cloud - ed
of - ten   and   view   our   acts   as

by   the   Fall,   we   are   at   a
dev - il - ish   when   we   try   for

loss   to   com - pre - hend   his
good,   let   us   be   gra - cious

155

Stead - fast Love, gra - cious - ly com -
to them all, hard hearts let us

mand - ing we love each oth - er,
soft - en, and seek our neigh - bors

as a - bove he doth from the Cross.
to re - call to our broth - er - hood.

Saint Cadoc

A Celebration
of Sacrifice

september 25
---
commemoration of saint cadoc

saint cadoc

Saint Cadoc lived in the early sixth century and founded one of the main churches in Wales at Llancarfan. According to the legends, he traveled extensively and tirelessly through the Celtic lands, establishing churches and monasteries from Brittany to Scotland. Often, these were associated in the stories with fantastic miracles; for example, his prayers were said to have restored a bridge from the mainland to an island monastery in Brittany, and he reputedly spoke with a dead giant in Scotland. Of course, such stories, while they may have had some significant metaphorical meaning, can hardly be taken at face value.

The extant record, however, shows only fifteen dedications in Wales and one in Cornwall. While sixteen is certainly a respectable number for one clergyman to have founded, the need for hyperbole in describing his life – rife with conflicts against a pride-filled Arthur and even a miraculous translation to Benevento – suggests that this was a saint about whom there was something very special, but not something that would lend itself to an acceptably extensive story. Indeed, to build up his story, his hagiographers included elements of Celtic folklore perhaps even a bit more blatantly than they did for most of the other saints.

The remarkable thing about Saint Cadoc's actual life appears to be in his manner of death. The story goes that he was given a choice by an angel: Either he could die peacefully (as did most of the major British saints whose names we have recorded) or he could die violently – but while celebrating the mass. This would appear to pose a greater question: Did he love his God and the people of his God enough to give his life as a priest in the very service of the Eucharist, the holy rite connecting God and humanity?

Saint Cadoc chose the form of death that was at once the more violent and the more highly dedicated to the Peace. As he was performing the Eucharist, into the church strode a soldier – perhaps a pagan invader or a Briton in the service of a lord who feared Cadoc's following in the church. The soldier drew his sword and beheaded the saint at the altar.

the symbol

Sacrifice has always been a part of Christianity, for it was in his free act of giving his life that we might find Life in him that Jesus became the Christ. And it was in his Resurrection that the sacrifice was made complete – the sacred healing deed. No matter how great we might suffer, so long as that suffering is in the Name of Christ, we shall never lose the eternal Life he has promised. Thus, the symbol for Saint Cadoc has four daggers pressed into the very heart of the cross. Yet, although the daggers may thrust right through the wheel of humanity to cause death in this life, the thread of eternal Life within the cross is never severed.

liturgy of the word

holy scripture

And Stephen, full of grace and power, did great wonders and signs among the people. Then some of those who belonged to the synagogue of the Freemen (as it was called), and of the Cyrenians, and of the Alexandrians, and of those from Cilicia and Asia, arose and disputed with Stephen. But they could not withstand the wisdom and the Spirit with which he spoke. Then they secretly instigated men, who said, "We have heard him speak blasphemous words against Moses and God." And they stirred up the people and the elders and the scribes, and they came upon him and seized him, and brought him before the council, and set up false witnesses who said, "This man never ceases to speak words against this holy place and the law; for we have heard him say that this Jesus of Nazareth will destroy this place, and will change the customs which Moses delivered to us." And gazing at him, all who sat in the council saw that his face was like the face of an angel.

. . .

Now when they heard these things they were enraged, and they ground their teeth against him. But he, full of the Holy Spirit, gazed into heaven and saw the glory of God, and Jesus standing at the right hand of God; and he said "Behold, I see the heavens opened, and the Son of man standing at the right hand of God." But they cried out with a loud voice and stopped their ears and rushed together upon him. Then they cast him out of the city and stoned him; and the witnesses laid down their garments at the feet of a young man named Saul. And as they were stoning Stephen, he prayed, "Lord Jesus, receive my spirit." And he knelt down and cried with a loud voice, "Lord, do not hold this sin against them." And when he had said this, he fell asleep. (Acts 6:8-15 – 7:54-60)

meðitation

How much are we willing to sacrifice for God and his people? Today, it is doubtful that any of us would be called upon to lay down our lives as martyrs to his service, as Saint Stephen and many others did in the early Church. But there are sacrifices that we may well be called upon to make very frequently. For even in the nominally Christian lands, the Word of God is not well received by the "Opponents" – those inclined to violence and those who value their worldly power above all else, even above human life.

What do we do when we are surrounded by the Opponents? We are at a meeting of the board of a large corporation that stands to make a great profit – at the expense of many people. Perhaps it is a food corporation that sees profits in reducing the nutritional value in baby food, putting children at risk. Perhaps it is a land development corporation that sees profits in driving poor people from their homes in order to build an amusement park or a golf course for the wealthy. Perhaps it is an armament corporation that sees profits in selling weapons to both sides in a civil war and in publishing propaganda to prolong that war.

So there we sit at a table among the powerful and the rich. What would happen if we said that these profits are not worth the harm done to the people of God? What would happen if, there in the midst of the Opponents, we steadfastly refused to cooperate in a venture that would be contrary to the Steadfast Love of Christ? At the very least, we could lose our livelihoods, our families and friends could reject us as insane, we could be branded as unfit for future employment.

Is this what Jesus calls upon us to do when he says: "If any man would come after me, let him deny himself and take up his cross and follow me. For whoever would save his life will lose it; and whoever loses his life for my sake and the gospel's will save it. For what does it profit a man, to gain the whole world and forfeit his life? For what can a man give in return for his life? For whoever is ashamed of me and of my words in this adulterous and sinful generation, of him will the Son of man also be ashamed, when he comes in the glory of his Father with the holy angels" (Mark 8:34b-38)?

All of a sudden, this time and this land do not appear to be so "Christian" anymore. We are surrounded by Opponents who could do us real harm in direct, but also in subtle ways. We could become poor powerless outcasts by holding to the Word of God.

Nor do we have to be members of some large corporation to feel the threat of extreme sacrifice for our Lord. The very same thing can happen in a town council meeting, at a university, or even in a church. Indeed, what would happen if we saw that a project our church wanted to take up to raise funds would harm other people or would otherwise be contrary to the teachings of Christ? Would we find it worth the ostracism of our friends, family, and fellow parishioners to speak up?

Yes, we are called to sacrifice more often than we probably care to notice. But once we hear that dreaded call, what do we do?

liturgy of prayer

collect

All sacrificing God, who hast given thine only Son and thy very self for us, that we might live at thy precious cost: Let us not forget the gift of life that thou hast given us, nor let us shrink from placing this gift in service to thee without weighing the cost to us; through Jesus Christ our Lord, who liveth and reigneth with thee and the Holy Spirit, one God, for ever and ever. *Amen.*

hymn: saint cadoc

Stand by us, Lord, lest we should falter
in our accord with thee and thy Word.
Let us not shy from thy great altar,
nor thee deny from fear of the sword.

Stand by us, Lord, give us the daring
to stay aboard though seas swell around.
Teach us to dare, thy Name declaring,
standing in prayer and holding our ground.

Stand by us, Lord, keeping us ever
true to thy Word, in spite of the threat
that people make in their endeavor
that we forsake our oath and our debt.

Stand by us, Lord, let not our pallor
weaken our word; but give us thy strength
that to the end with steadfast valor,
we may contend whatever the length.

thanksgiving

We thank thee, Lord, that thou hast given us the example of Saint
Cadoc to guide us to a more perfect sacrifice in thee.

grace

Almighty and everliving God, by thy Grace let us not shrink from the
sacrifice of Cadoc.

Saint Cadoc

Gently

1. Stand   by   us,   Lord,
2. Stand   by   us,   Lord,
3. Stand   by   us,   Lord,
4. Stand   by   us,   Lord,

lest   we   should   fal - ter
give   us   the   dar - ing
keep - ing   us   ev - er
let   not   our   pal - lor

in   our   ac -   cord   with
to   stay   a-   board   though
true   to   thy   Word,   in
weak - en   our   word;   but

thee   and   thy   Word.
seas   swell   a -   round.
spite   of   the   threat
give   us   thy   strength

Let   us   not   shy
Teach   us   to   dare,
that   peo -   ple   make
that   to   the   end

166

from   thy   great al -   tar,
thy   Name   de - clar -   ing,
in   their   en - deav -   or
with stead -   fast val -   or,

nor   thee   de -   ny   from
stand - ing   in prayer   and
that   we   for - sake   our
we   may   con - tend   what -

fear   of   the sword.
hold - ing   our ground.
oath   and   our debt.
ev -   er   the length.

167

Saint Ia

A Celebration
of Persistence

octoben 27
(also februany 3)
---
commemoration of saint ia

saint ia

Saint Ia (or Hya) is the patron of St Ives in Cornwall. She belonged to one of those wondering bands of missionaries that traveled from one Celtic land to another, making converts, sharing news and innovations, establishing churches and monasteries, and tying the Celtic Church together into a loosely organized but tightly interrelated network – indeed, a Celtic knotwork – of devout Christians.

The sister of Saint Euny (another of the patron saints in Cornwall) and the daughter of a noble Irish family, she sailed to Cornwall from Ireland in the late fifth or early sixth century with several monks, reported to include Saints Gwinear, Fingar, and Piala. After establishing a church through the authority of a local chieftain named Dinan and after performing much missionary activity with her group, she once again set sail to the south, traveling with 777 missionaries to Brittany. There she was martyred in the service of our Lord.

The story of Saint Ia revolves around these two major trips in her mission. She was evidently a very small person, and perhaps her companions did not feel that she was able to make the arduous voyage between Ireland and Cornwall. Whatever the reason, she was left behind on the beach. After a series of ordeals (that the later Life of Saint Gwinear generously embellishes), she followed her fellow missionaries to Cornwall.

Again, in the voyage of the 777 she was left behind. And once again, not willing to be separated from her mission, she miraculously made her way to Brittany alone. The legend has it that as she prayed on the beach, she saw a leaf that grew large enough for her to sail. Perhaps this reflects her small stature, but the story is certainly influenced by folklore. It is more likely that she spied a small boat, and rather than being left on the shore, she braved the Channel on her own.

Such persistence is the mark of Saint Ia. She refused to be separated from her mission, from her companions, from her Lord. With steadfast faith she dared whatever danger might come her way to maintain the connections so important to the Celtic Church and indeed to all of Christianity.

the symbol

Although Saint Ia was a small person, the path she followed was long and complicated. It wove and turned; and just when one pattern emerged and the road appeared to be predictable, the pattern shifted and once again there was bewilderment. Yet, if we follow the path with the persistence of Saint Ia, we will eventually discover that so long as we remain within the cross, we cannot be lost. For the cross of our Lord Jesus Christ is the Way, in which everyone is connected through him. But at any one turn, we cannot see that the path leads us back; nor can we be assured that we shall not be lost. Such assurance we derive not from our own knowledge, but only from our faith in God and his Steadfast Love for us.

liturgy of the word

holy scripture

Who shall separate us from the love of Christ? Shall tribulation, or distress, or persecution, or famine, or nakedness, or peril, or sword? As it is written,
> "For thy sake we are being killed all the day long;
> we are regarded as sheep to be slaughtered."

No, in all these things we are more than conquerors through him who loved us. For I am sure that neither death, nor life, nor angels, nor principalities, nor things present, nor things to come, nor powers, nor height, nor depth, nor anything else in all creation, will be able to separate us from the love of God in Christ Jesus our Lord. (Romans 8:35-39)

meditation

One of the most frightening experiences we have all shared as children is to be separated from our parents. No matter how careful the loving parents may be, and no matter how desperately the fearful child clings, there comes the moment – if only for seconds – that the child looks around and in panic cannot see the parents.

Perhaps we can recall the feeling. We are in a crowd of giants, whom we do not know and whom we do not want to know. Maybe they are good, and maybe they are evil – again, we do not know. All we do know is that they are separating us from our parents. We are alone and helpless. We are abandoned and forlorn. We are hopelessly

172

lost and doomed. We cry out in anguish to our parents, but they do not hear.

This is indeed how we felt – how children always feel when they inevitably find themselves in this situation. Without the perspective of age, they do not realize that their loneliness and hopelessness will last only a moment and that their parents are really not far away at all. Their vision is limited to a small world with giant obstacles.

And so it is with us. We are left behind in life, alone and without the Steadfast Love of God. We know this because the obstacles we face are so great that we cannot possibly overcome them. We are hopelessly lost and doomed, abandoned and forlorn, alone and helpless. We face giant obstacles, giant opponents, giant failures.

Just as the child's vision is limited compared to that of an adult, so is our vision limited compared to that of our heavenly Father. God knows where we are; God knows what we are going through; God knows how desperate we feel. He loves us with a Steadfast Love and will never ever abandon us, no matter how much we believe in our panic that he is gone.

But if God has not lost us, then why do we feel so alone? The fact that the parents may look across the room and see the "lost" child does not make the child feel any less lost. The child must see the parents – must become aware that the parents are there. So how do we become aware of the ever-presence of God?

We become aware of God, we gain the assurance that he is with us, when we pray. But we cannot become aware of him when we simply recite by mindless rote the prayers we learned in childhood. That is as helpful as the lost child's cries – the cries that are invariably so loud that the child cannot even hear the parents when they call back to the child with reassurance.

To feel the connection that God faithfully maintains with us, we must prayerfully listen. Once the din of our own crying and panic subsides, we will feel the reassurance of God soothing and comforting us. For no matter how much we panic, how much we doubt, how much we despair, nothing can separate us from the love of God which is in Christ Jesus our Lord.

In order to gain the reassurance that our God loves us with a steadfast and never ending love (a love we receive without condition, as the love the good parent gives to the child), we must persistently refuse to allow anything to separate us from our love of God.

liturgy of prayer

collect

Ever persistently steadfast God, from whose love we are incapable of being separated: Grant us such a Spirit that we might love thee with such obstinate persistence that we may never suffer that faulty and faithless perception that would lead us to fear that thou art not with us; through Jesus Christ our Lord, who liveth and reigneth with thee and the Holy Spirit, one God, for ever and ever. *Amen.*

hymn: saint ia

The Lord is always with his flock;
he is the true eternal rock.
With Steadfast Love he standeth fast
against life's chill and stormy blast.

Though without failing he doth stand
behind us on life's shifting sand,
how often we forget our Lord,
neglecting to share in his Word.

Forgive us, Lord, that we forget
to stand with thee, our hearts to set
upon thine all persistent love
that floweth to us from above.

Lord, give us but a small degree
of thy persistent love, that we
might stand by thee in constant trust
and do those things we know we must.

thanksgiving

We thank thee, Lord, that thou hast given us the example of Saint Ia
to guide us to a more perfect persistence in thee.

grace

Almighty and everliving God, by thy Grace let persist with Ia in seeking
to do thy will.

Saint Ia

1. The Lord is al - ways
2. For - give us, Lord, that

with his flock; he is the true e -
we for - get to stand with thee, our

ter - nal rock. With Stead - fast Love he
hearts to set u - pon thine all per -

stand - eth fast a - gainst life's chill and
sist - ent love that flow - eth to us

storm - y blast. Though with - out fail - ing
from a - bove. Lord, give us but a

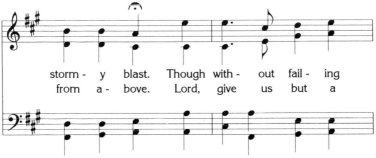

177

he doth stand be - hind us on life's
small de - gree of thy per - sist - tent

shift - ing sand, how of - ten we for -
love, that we might stand by thee in

get our Lord, ne- glect - ing to share in his Word.
con- stant trust and do those things we know we must.

178

Saint Hildutus

A Celebration

of Learning

november 6
---
commemoration of saint hildutus

saint hildutus

Saint Hildutus served God in the second half of the fifth century and died early in the sixth. He is better known by his Welsh name Illtud (or Illtyd) and by his Breton name Eltut; and his relationship with Wales and Brittany is intimate and complex.

According to one tradition, he was a Breton soldier who traveled to Britain to aid in the wars. A divine revelation impelled him to seek ordination and he became abbot of Llanilltud Fawr (Llantwit Major) in Morganwg (Glamorgan), Wales. In this tradition, he was apparently a successful and powerful military figure, in line for fame and riches. His revelation can thus be seen as one of those traditional "afflictions" that humbles one's position as it enriches one's heart.

In the other tradition (which is inherently more credible if only because it is more mundane), his connection between the two countries goes in the other direction. As abbot of the monastery, he sailed to Brittany with food and medical supplies to help out these displaced Britons in a famine. Such a story would reflect the enriched heart of one who has through revelation been convinced of the saving grace of the church.

Of course, given the frequent and close contact between Britain and its colony in Brittany, it is entirely possible that there is truth in both traditions. The fact is that there are numerous church dedications to him both in Wales and in Brittany. Whether he ever was a soldier or not, these dedications in both countries would certainly indicate that his clerical duties spanned the Channel.

We can tell from his associations in various Lives and from his highly influential position as abbot of Llanilltud Fawr – a very important monastery that even bears his name – that Saint Hildutus was one of the foremost figures in the British Church of the Dark Ages. He is mentioned prominently with such saints as Dubricius, David, and Samson, and in a Life of Saint Samson he is referred to as the disciple of Saint Germanus of Auxerre (the details of which, while factually in doubt, serve to illustrate how highly he was regarded).

One characteristic of Saint Hildutus that we can accept with absolute confidence was his love of learning. The very foundation of Llanilltud Fawr evidences this dedication to learning not only of Scripture, but of secular philosophy as well. Nor was his drive to learn just some idle avocation of a monk looking for something to do. Rather, he delved into Scripture and philosophy to find their application to the Life in Christ, and he spread his learning abroad throughout Britain and Brittany.

the symbol

At the head, the arms, and the foot of the cross are Trinity knots. The Grace of the Trinity flows from the head of Christ, from his thoughts and soul; the Grace of the Trinity flows from the arms of Christ, from his works and from his embracing of us all; the Grace of the Trinity flows from the foot of Christ, from the foundation of the faith in his Holy Church. All of this Grace flows into the center of the cross, the heart of a cross of love. And at the heart is the Wisdom knot. This knot is different from the common Solomon knot of knowledge that is represented by two interlocking links, for the Solomon knot is not interconnected. Knowledge without Wisdom does not bind anything together. Wisdom, on the other hand, is the Sophia of Christ and it binds many things – indeed, all things.

181

liturgy of the word

holy scripture

Thou hast dealt well with thy servant,
    O LORD, according to thy word.
Teach me good judgement and knowledge,
    for I believe in thy commandments.
Before I was afflicted I went astray;
    but now I keep thy word.
Thou art good and doest good;
    teach me thy statutes.
The godless besmear me with lies,
    but with my whole heart I keep thy precepts;
their heart is gross like fat,
    but I delight in thy law.
It is good for me that I was afflicted,
    that I might learn thy statutes.
The law of thy mouth is better to me
    than thousands of gold and silver pieces.
                (Psalm 119:65-72 – *Teth*)

meditation

    We tend to be far more comfortable in ignorance than in knowledge, especially when we consider our ignorance to be knowledge. Ignorance shores up our preconceptions and keeps us from having to go through the turmoil of changing our ways. Knowledge, on the other hand, challenges us to make changes that may well be uncomfortable and even threatening.

182

This is especially true of both ignorance and knowledge of Holy Scripture. Let us consider the following often-cited verse from the Second Epistle from Saint Paul to the Church in Thessalonica: "For even when we were with you, we gave you this command: If any one will not work, let him not eat" (2 Thessalonians 3:10).

How opportune a verse this is if we do not want to care for the poor. If our neighbor is unemployed and destitute, we simply have to say that Saint Paul instructs us that if you do not work, you do not eat. Thus, it is not our fault that our neighbor is hungry; it is our neighbor's fault for not working. The Bible tells us so.

For our own Christianity, one of the saddest things about taking an attitude like this is that we feel confident in our righteousness. We are in a right relationship with God even though we allow our neighbor to suffer (in itself an impossible contradiction), because we are doing God's will as it is stated in Scripture. We feel smug and contented in this apparent righteousness. And if we do feel some pang of guilt over our neighbor's condition, we can even turn it into a matter of not being our sin, but our neighbor's. By being hungry, our neighbor is sinful and must therefore deserve to suffer.

Yet, if we read more in the Bible, our new knowledge will displace our old ignorance in a most humiliating manner. If we just read the next verse, we learn: "For we hear that some of you are living in idleness, mere busybodies, not doing any work" (2 Thessalonians 3:11). Those who are not working and thus deserve not to eat are far from unemployed and destitute. They are failing to work because they are going about pretentiously judging others – perhaps being as pretentiously judgmental as we were when we condemned our hungry neighbor for not working.

Moreover, if we study the Scriptures further to include the reasons for Saint Paul's letter to the Church in Thessolonica, we will be further humbled. There were members of the church who were not working because they thought that the end of the world was so imminent that there was no need to work – there would be no tomorrow. Saint Paul's admonition, therefore, had nothing to do with the morality of working for our food.

If we go beyond this epistle and study all of the Scriptures, our learning will humble us once again – and even more thoroughly.

Throughout both testaments God the Father, the prophets, and Jesus all demand consistently that those who are hungry must be fed. This was the very basis of the communal nature of the Hebrew Law, and troubles came to Israel whenever the poor, the hungry, and the alien were ignored.

In the Hebrew Law, our duty to the poor is spelled out explicitly: "If there is among you a poor man, one of your brethren, in any of your towns within your land which the LORD your God gives you, you shall not harden your heart or shut your hand against your poor brother, but you shall open your hand to him, and lend him sufficient for his need, whatever it may be. . . . For the poor will never cease out of the land; therefore I command you, You shall open wide your hand to your brother, to the needy and to the poor, in the land" (Deuteronomy 15:7-8, 11).

This tradition is echoed and magnified in the words of our Lord Jesus Christ, who describes the righteous and the saved: "for I was hungry and you gave me food, I was thirsty and you gave me drink, I was a stranger and you welcomed me, I was naked and you clothed me, I was sick and you visited me, I was in prison and you came to me" (Matthew 25:35-36).

Once we gain knowledge to replace our ignorance, we are humbled in the realization that we have not acted according to the Word. Nor can we ever go back to that former blissful state of ignorance, pretending not to have heard or understood the knowledge from Holy Scripture. Such feigned ignorance is summarized in the words of the proverbialist: "A righteous man knows the rights of the poor; a wicked man does not understand such knowledge" (Proverbs 29:7).

Such is the burden that learning places upon us. And yet, learning is also a release from a far greater burden. When we know what to do and we do it, we are freed from guilt.

"And you will know the truth, and the truth will make you free" (John 8:32).

184

liturgy of prayer

collect

All knowing and understanding God, who offerest us thy learning to free us from guilt and thy truth to guide our feet in the paths of righteousness: Grant that we may read and understand thy Holy Scripture and all the knowledge that thou hast made for us in the thoughts, the words, and the deeds of thy people to the end that our actions may be pleasing both to thee and to our neighbor; through Jesus Christ our Lord, who liveth and reigneth with thee and the Holy Spirit, one God, for ever and ever. *Amen.*

hymn: saint hildutus

Wisdom and Light in the works of the Lord
shine through the darkness to show us the Way,
leading to Truth in his infinite Word,
guiding us to an eternal new Day.

Heaven and earth, harken to his command!
Silently yield up to his holy Truth!
Age's experience cannot withstand,
nor can the heat of impetuous youth.

All must acknowledge the Lord's holy Word,
learning from him what our minds can discern,
calling on him with one urgent accord –
that he might teach us his Wisdom to learn.

thanksgiving

We thank thee, Lord, that thou hast given us the example of Saint Hildutus to guide us to a more perfect learning in thee.

grace

Almighty and everliving God, by thy Grace let us strive with the enthusiasm of Hildutus to learn thy statutes and to live by them.

Saint Hildutus

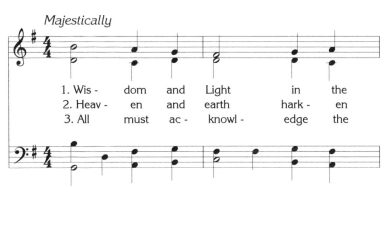

Majestically

1. Wis - dom and Light in the
2. Heav - en and earth hark - en
3. All must ac - knowl - edge the

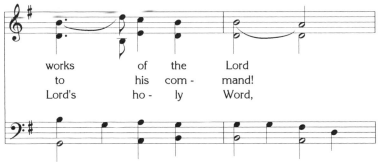

works of the Lord
to his com - mand!
Lord's ho - ly Word,

shine through the dark - ness to
Si - lent - ly yield up to
learn - ing from him what our

show us the Way,
his ho - ly Truth!
minds can dis - cern,

lead - ing to Truth in his
A - ge's ex - per - i - ence
call - ing on him with one

188

in - fin - ite Word,
can - not with - stand,
ur - gent ac - cord --

guid - ing us to an e -
nor can the heat of im -
that he might teach us his

ter - nal new Day.
pet - u - ous youth.
Wis - dom to learn.

189

Saint Dubricius

A Celebration

of Light

november 14
---
commemoration of
saint dubricius

saint dubricius

Saint Dubricius (or Dyfrig in Welsh) flourished during the first half of the sixth century. From what few reliable records we have and from the distribution of churches bearing his name, he appears to have been a very active abbot/bishop in the area around Hereford. However, church dedications go far beyond this region into Wales and were probably at one time more prevalent in what has since become England as well.

Although little is known about him, he is one of the most tantalizing figures in Dark Ages Britain. Given his rather broad area of influence, we can deduce that he was an extraordinarily important cleric in the British Church. Supporting this view is the fact that he comes down to us in later records not simply as Saint Dubricius, but as Papa Dubricius. Indeed, in the Life of Saint Samson (written relatively early) he is portrayed as a bishop who consecrated other bishops (and that in a Life that is not even dedicated to him). It is no wonder that in later (though less reliable) legends he is described as an archbishop – in fact, the Archbishop of Britain. Certainly the title Papa (well after the title was no longer used for priests in general) would imply a position within the loosely confederated British Church roughly equivalent to Patriarch.

While the later legends are notoriously unreliable, his importance for the Church is certainly evident in them. Indeed, when Arthur was elevated in legend to high king or emperor, it was assumed that Saint Dubricius must have presided over the coronation. In order to increase that church's already considerable prestige, the church at Llandaf inserted in his biography his that he had been bishop there.

And even more fascinating little details seem to survive in the Lives and indicate a pervasive influence on British legend. Various scholars have made more or less credible conjectures, though we cannot really tell much for sure. One such detail is a passing reference that while he was abbot in Hereford, he spent some time fishing in the River Wye. The setting in which he is described seems to suggest one root source for the developing legend of the Fisher King.

Certainly given his prominence, his wide-ranging influence, his consecration of bishops, and his enigmatic title of Papa, one description of Saint Dubricius is entirely fitting and most likely historical – he was "as a candle on a stand." He stood high above the landscape and provided light to all the Britons in their tragic siege by the Germanic hordes and the Gaelic pirates and in the internal political deterioration that was to be the Britons' undoing.

the symbol

Saint Dubricius was "as a candle on a stand." The candle contains the design from the Chalice of Ardagh (Ireland) and represents Christ (the Greek letter Chi, resembling an X) in the center connected with his twelve Apostles (the twelve knots). At the top of the candle is the Flame of Pentecost, the Holy Spirit that descended upon the Apostles and lit the Way for them. The stand is the Celtic cross, for the Light rests upon the Steadfast Love of God made manifest in the sacrifice of his only begotten Son, our Savior Jesus Christ. The steps at the foot of the cross/stand are a traditional symbol for the world – the world that erected the cross to crucify our Lord, and the world which our Lord Christ has taken to be his base.

193

liturgy of the word

holy scripture

You are the light of the world. A city set on a hill cannot be hid. Nor do men light a lamp and put it under a bushel, but on a stand, and it gives light to all in the house. Let your light so shine before men, that they may see your good works and give glory to your Father who is in heaven. (Matthew 5:14-16)

And we have the prophetic word made more sure. You will do well to pay attention to this as to a lamp shining in a dark place, until the day dawns and the morning star rises in your hearts. (2 Peter 1:19)

In the beginning was the Word, and the Word was with God, and the Word was God. He was in the beginning with God; all things were made through him, and without him was not anything made that was made. In him was life, and the life was the light of men. The light shines in the darkness and the darkness has not overcome it. (John 1:1-5)

meditation

We are in pitch darkness and can see nothing. There are noises around us, but we cannot tell what they are or where they come from. Is it some predatory animal stalking us, ready to pounce at any

194

moment? Is it an enemy who somehow can see us and is preparing to kill us? We are completely helpless and totally at the mercy of the darkness.

But then we hear the voice of a friend quite near us. He tells us not to move, for if we move on our own in the darkness, we do not know what manner of danger we might walk into. Our friend lights a match close to the ground, guarding it gently with his hands until it glows steadily. Carefully, he brings a candle to the match and, still guarding the precious flame with his hands, he lights the wick.

Now we have light, but we cannot see very far. Our friend slowly and carefully raises the candle. As he raises it, we see clearly the ground right around us; and we see the reflections of evil-looking eyes retreating into the darkness. Our friend places the candle on a tall stand and lifts it high, illuminating the land all around.

And we see more candles. With great relief we rush to gather them and touch their wicks to the flaming wick of our friend. Now we can fan out and chase away the darkness and the evil that has surrounded us.

Our Friend is Jesus, and he is the Light that saves us and assures us, saying, "I am the light of the world; he who follows me will not walk in darkness, but will have the light of life" (John 8:12b). In tearful joy we sing to the Lord "Thy word is a lamp to my feet and a light to my path" (Psalm 119:105).

This is the Light that the Prophet Isaiah spoke of: "Then shall your light break forth like the dawn, and your healing shall spring up speedily; your righteousness shall go before you, the glory of the LORD shall be your rear guard" (Isaiah 58:8) and "Your sun shall no more go down, nor your moon withdraw itself; for the LORD will be your everlasting light, and your days of mourning shall be ended" (Isaiah 60:20).

Jesus assures us that as long as he is in the world, he shall be the Light the world. And at Whitsuntide he passed on his Light to his disciples: "And there appeared to them tongues as of fire, distributed and resting on each one of them" (Acts 2:3). Thus has the Holy Spirit been passed on through the very darkest of the ages.

The saints have passed on this flame to us, that we might also be as candles on a stand for Christ. With the fire that we have received through the hardships of many generations, we push back the darkness and chase away the creatures of evil.

But this is not an easy task. We know the terror of being in the darkness and at the mercy of the creatures of darkness. To push back the darkness, we must take our candles on their stands and walk toward this fearsome void. Armed with the Light, however, we know that no Darkness can prevail: "The light shines in the darkness, and the darkness has not overcome it."

liturgy of prayer

collect

Everliving and ever shining God, who hast given us the one true Light through thine only true and adorable Son Jesus Christ: Grant us the courage and the will to take up this Light as candles on a stand, that we might bring the Light of Life into the world to the Glory of our Lord and Savior Jesus Christ; through the same Jesus Christ our Lord, who liveth and reigneth with thee and the Holy Spirit, one God, for ever and ever. *Amen.*

hymn: saint dubricius

Grant us, oh Lord, thy flame to bear
into the darkness drear.
Lead us with boldness to declare
thy saving Grace is near.

Grant us, oh Lord, that we may be
as candles on a stand,
spreading thy Gospel joyously
through all the darkened land.

And in the end let us pass on
thy flame to souls unborn;
till at the last, thy victory won,
our darkness turns to morn.

thanksgiving

We thank thee, Lord, that thou hast given us the example of Saint Dubricius to guide us to a more perfect light in thee.

grace

Almighty and everliving God, by thy Grace let us like Dubricius be a light to the world around us.

Saint Dubricius

drear.   Lead   us   with   bold - ness
stand,   spread - ing   thy   Gos - pel
born;   till   at   the   last,   thy

to   de - clare   thy   sav - ing   Grace   is
joy - ous - ly   through   all   the   dark - ened
vic - tory   won,   our   dark - ness   turns   to

near.
land.
morn.

199

Saint Samthann

A Celebration
of Spirituality

december 18
---
commemoration of
saint samthann

saint samthann

By the time of Saint Samthann (or Safan), who died in the year 739, the great age of Celtic Spirituality had already passed, although the Dark Ages would continue. Yet she embodied this spirituality to such a degree that the leaders of the Celi-Dé (or the Culdees – a reform movement that sought to reintroduce the old spirit into the Irish Church) sought her out and wrote down her considerable advice and wisdom. Although she was highly regarded and was constantly offered gifts of land and livestock, she chose rather to live simply and in poverty in her nunnery. As for her gift of spiritual wisdom, she gave in to no pretensions, but spoke her mind simply in the humility of Christian equality.

Her foster father was an Irish king and arranged a marriage for her with a powerful nobleman. Before the marriage could be consummated, however, she had a fiery vision of the Holy Spirit so intense that others saw it as well, and she chose to give herself rather in marriage to God. The vision of fire associated with the Holy Spirit and visible to others seems to be a mark of Saint Samthann, for she was called from her monastery and made abbess of Clonbroney because of a dream by Saint Funecha in which Samthann engulfed the monastery in the benevolent flame of the Spirit.

Such visions are quite fitting for her, for the spiritual light is a symbol of goodness and wisdom. She took personal charge of the finances in her monastery, not to ensure increase of her coffers, but instead to be certain that as much was given to the sick and the poor as possible.

In spiritual wisdom she is perhaps the most prominent of all the Irish saints. Her friendship and advice were sought from every corner of the Island, making her the most famous of the Celtic "soul friends." Most of this advice had to do with prayer. When asked in what position we should pray, she replied that we should pray in every position – in fact, we should never cease praying no matter whatever else we may be doing. When asked if we are required to go on a pilgrimage for God, she replied that God is everywhere, anyway, and is nearest when we call to him in prayer.

To Saint Samthann, however, prayer and even spirituality were not to be isolated from one's daily round, nor from learning. When a friend told her that he was going to give up his studying in order to devote himself entirely to prayer, she advised against it. After all, she maintained, if he did not study, upon what would he fix his mind to enable him to pray? It was not enough simply to engage in prayer: Saint Samthan would have people learn so they would know what they were praying about.

the symbol

The symbol of Saint Samthann captures the essence of her teachings about spirituality. If we are to be connected with the cross of the love of Jesus Christ, we must join both our hearts and our minds together through that cross – through our dedication to the love and the sacrifice of our Lord. The heart, representing the Steadfast Love of our God through Christ, thus flows into the cross as the cross flows into it. Likewise, the Wisdom knot, representing not simply knowledge by itself, but the divine Sophia of God expressed through the Resurrection of Christ Jesus, flows into the cross as the cross flows into it. Spirituality blossoms when our hearts and minds are joined through love.

liturgy of the word

holy scripture

There are doubtless many different languages in the world, and none is without meaning; but if I do not know the meaning of the language, I shall be a foreigner to the speaker and the speaker a foreigner to me. So with yourselves; since you are eager for manifestations of the Spirit, strive to excel in building up the church.

Therefore, he who speaks in a tongue should pray for the power to interpret. For if I pray in a tongue, my spirit prays but my mind is unfruitful. What am I to do? I will pray with the spirit and I will pray with the mind also; I will sing with the spirit and I will sing with the mind also. Otherwise, if you bless with the spirit, how can any one in the position of an outsider say the "Amen" to your thanksgiving when he does not know what you are saying? For you may give thanks well enough, but the other man is not edified. I thank God that I speak in tongues more than you all; nevertheless, in church I would rather speak five words with my mind, in order to instruct others, than ten thousand words in a tongue. (1 Corinthians 14:10-19)

204

meditation

As the world grows smaller, ever fewer of us have not experienced hearing a foreign language we do not understand. Perhaps the speaker is looking right at us and speaking with great urgency, doubtless trying to communicate something of importance to us both. Yet, try as we may, we cannot understand.

Surely, this is one of the most frustrating situations we can find ourselves in. The more urgently the foreigner speaks to us, the more desperately we want and need to comprehend. We are two people who need to establish a bond, and indeed we may very well feel a bond in the urgency of the uncomprehended message – a bond between two human beings sharing a common frustration and knowing that somehow our lives are connected in ways we just cannot fathom.

The only way out of this problem is through learning. No matter how strongly we feel a bond growing between us, we cannot strengthen this bond if the foreigner does not learn enough of our language and if we do not learn enough of the foreign language to allow us to communicate.

And so it is among us all and between us and God whenever we come together to pray. We have learned many prayers, hymns, and psalms in our childhood, and they flow like honey from our lips Sunday after Sunday. Some of our prayers we recite in an archaic form of our language which we do not fully understand. What are we then communicating with God and with one another (for our prayers are certainly meant for our community as well)? What indeed are we communicating with ourselves if we cannot interpret what we say?

If we do not even understand the language we pray in, we are praying "in a tongue," as Saint Paul would put it. In effect, by reciting prayers that we do not understand and that we probably do not listen to anyway, we speak a foreign language with our own spirit.

Sometimes in our prayers, we say words we understand, but they do not communicate with us. In our most widely recited psalm, we declare "The LORD is my shepherd; I shall not want. He makes me lie down in green pastures. He leads me beside still waters" (Psalm 23:1-

2). If we know little about sheep, we will probably miss the importance of the waters being still – a detail that speaks directly to the goodness of the Shepherd.

If we do not understand our prayers to God and the prayers of our community, how can we establish a true relationship with God and with each other? Spirituality requires the effort of study.

liturgy of prayer

collect

Most generous God, who hast given us a spirit to pray, a mind to communicate, and a soul to contain them both: Give unto us a desire for learning that we might know what we should say to thee and to comprehend what thou dost say to us; and give us a will to pray unceasingly with thee that our spirits and thy Spirit may become one; through Jesus Christ our Lord, who liveth and reigneth with thee and the Holy Spirit, one God, for ever and ever. *Amen.*

hymn: saint samthann

Reveal thyself to us, oh Christ,
as thou hast done before,
when thou thyself once sacrificed,
our spirits to restore.

We cannot know thy holy Way,
if thou dost not reveal
thy mysteries, for who can say
what lieth under seal?

Yet thou hast given us a mind
to contemplate thy Word.
In study we must seek to find
what truths can be inferred

from Holy Scripture and from thought
of saints and of the wise,
whose labor hath in someways brought
some light before our eyes.

So let us now our praises sing
in spirit and in truth
to God our high and gracious King
who in his boundless ruth

hath given us both mind and heart
that we may bind in one
both thought and soul in equal part
in holy unison.

thanksgiving

We thank thee, Lord, that thou hast given us the example of Saint
Samthann to guide us to a more perfect spirituality in thee.

grace

Almighty and everliving God, by thy Grace let us pray, learn, and live
with the spirituality of Samthann.

Saint Samthann

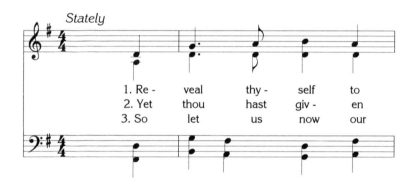

1. Re - veal thy - self to
2. Yet thou hast giv - en
3. So let us now our

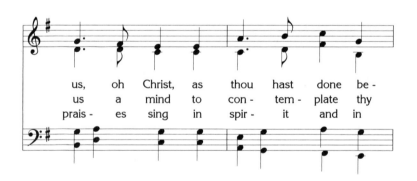

us, oh Christ, as thou hast done be -
us a mind to con - tem - plate thy
prais - es sing in spir - it and in

fore, when thou thy - self once
Word. In stud - y we must
truth to God our high and

sac - ri - ficed, our spir - its to re -
seek to find what truths can be in -
grac - ious King who in his bound - less

store. We can - not know thy
ferred from Ho - ly Scrip - ture
ruth hath giv - en us both

ho - ly Way, if thou dost not re -
and from thought of saints and of the
mind and heart that we may bind in

veal thy mys - ter - ies, for
wise, whose la - bor hath in
one both thought and soul in

who can say what li - eth un - der seal?
some - ways brought some light be - fore our eyes.
e - qual part, in ho - ly u - nis - on.

210

All Celtic Saints

A Celebration
of Dedication

november 1
---
commemoration of all celtic saints

all celtic saints

All Celtic Saints show us Christian qualities that we admire and lives we can try to emulate. Saint Patrick forgave those who had captured and enslaved him to the extent that he dedicated his life to winning his former captors over to Christ. Saint Brigid extended pure and all-encompassing love to those who called upon her, especially to the sick, the poor, and the hungry. Saint David demonstrated that we can all use our talents to convince others of the Way of Christ. Saint Dubricius was as a candle on a stand, shining forth the love of Christ through the darkest period in the history of the Western Isles.

Indeed, all of the saints in that tumultuous period of the Dark Ages were candles on a stand. And so they are still to us today. As we plod through our periods of darkness and despair as a church, or as individual members, we have but to look up to the Light as it is represented in these magnificent candles that stand in the presence of Christ and show us how mere mortals can reflect the Steadfast Love of God.

In many ways, the Christian tradition was saved by the saints of Britain and Ireland. As the migrating hordes of pagans swept through Europe, destroying monasteries and manuscripts and wreaking havoc on the people of God, the Celtic Church stood firm just long enough to ensure that all the people who came after could still find the Way.

Yet, as much as we honor such saints as Beuno, Monenna, Ciaran, and the rest whose names have survived the ages and whose lives are imperfectly known to us, we must not forget that these few saints were among thousands whose names we cannot recall but whose lives have passed Life on to us through their dedication: all the nuns and the monks who took in the famished and the wounded, all the bishops and the priests who administered the sacred rites to a besieged land, all the deacons who served the people of God in times of extreme danger from war and plague, all the baptized who held tenaciously onto their faith as catastrophe approached.

And so it is that on New Year's Day of the Celtic calendar – the first of November – we remember and honor All Saints.

the symbol

With All Celtic Saints we have reached the end and the beginning – the end of life and the beginning of Life. In the symbol for the Celtic Cross there were many knots in the wheel around the cross, representing the many people who live in the faith of God and who are connected through his Wisdom. Now the wheel is bare, for the knots have all been drawn by his Wisdom from the out-lying rim of humanity into the very cross itself. Wisdom is still at the center, but now so are we. Thus it is that we join as the people of God and accept his Grace in our life, so that we might achieve a more intimate Life through the love and sacrifice of our Lord Jesus Christ. And thus it is also that we fill out the cross as we fulfil the love of God. It is altogether fitting that this should be the New Year, as it is the New Life.

líturgy of the word

holy scripture

Let us now praise famous men
    and our fathers in their generations.
The Lord apportioned to them great glory,
    his majesty from the beginning.
There were those who ruled in their kingdoms
    and were men renowned for their power,
giving counsel by their understanding,
    and proclaiming prophecies;
leaders of the people in their deliberations
        and in understanding of learning for the people,
    wise in their words of instruction;
those who composed musical tunes,
    and set forth verses in writing;
rich men furnished with resources,
    living peaceably in their habitations —
all these were honored in their generations,
all were the glory of their times.
There are some of them who have left a name,
    so that men declare their praise.
And there are some who have no memorial,
    who have perished as though they had not lived;
they have become as though they had not been born,
    and so have their children after them.
But these were men of mercy,
    whose righteous deeds have not been forgotten;
their prosperity will remain with their descendants,

214

and their inheritance to their children's children.
Their descendants stand by the covenants;
    their children also, for their sake.
Their posterity will continue for ever,
    and their glory will not be blotted out.
Their bodies were buried in peace,
    and their name lives to all generations.
Peoples will declare their wisdom,
    and the congregation proclaims their praise.
                    (Ecclesiasticus 44:1-15)

meditation

We often feel that we stand at the end of an era, or even in a twilit time of uncertainty after the brightness of a bygone age. Before us have come the giants of humanity, who in the face of insuperable hardships accomplished great deeds – the deeds of heroes far beyond our meager abilities. And now we, with our impotence and fear, are faced by invincible forces that plot our destruction. We are doomed.

Those who study human behavior will say that such an attitude sells us short. Certainly, we are of the same stuff as the heroes who came before. They were great because they had an apparently insurmountable obstacle that they simply had to surmount. We are perfectly capable of doing the same thing, and what is more: Deep down within ourselves, we know it. Therefore, the argument goes, we should forget the heroes of yore – the saints whose accomplishments are vastly exaggerated, anyway – and set ourselves to our own tasks.

Essentially, this argument is sound up until the last sentence. As we prepare to make our own contributions to God, to the church, and to humanity, we cannot afford to ignore the saints and their heroic deeds, for in their "sacred healing deeds" (what the word *sacrifices* really means) they show us the way to accomplish our tasks and our very own identities.

Did Saint Nonna hold onto that rock, desperately clinging to her own life and to the life of the child she was to bear the next day for no other reason than to get through the night? No, her tenacity in clinging to that rock was a beacon to us all to cling to the Rock – to hold firmly onto our faith in God no matter what hardships and devastations might come our way – for we know that the dawn will bring a new Light and new Life, as surely as the Creator is steadfast in his love for us.

When it is our turn to cling to a rock in the midst of a storm of adversity (which surely will come), let us remember Saint Nonna. She has shown us the tenacity we need to accomplish our task, and she has shown us how very important it is that we do not loosen our grip – even if we wear that rock right down to a pebble.

For it is not true that the saints were only of their time and we are only of ours. Saint Nonna stands firmly at our side as we hold onto that rock. Saints Ciaran and Maedoc stand right there in front of us and implore us not to treat those who wish us ill with enmity, but to extend ourselves in friendship. Saint Brigid takes hold of our sleeve and pulls us back to the beggar we have just passed in the street. All the saints are with us every moment throughout all time, if only we will listen to them and follow them.

And if we dare to follow them down the paths they try to show us, then we shall be saints as well. This is what a saint is: a human being just like us who serves God as virtuously as he or she can.

There is an Age of Saints, and it is ours to enter if we dare.

liturgy of prayer

collect

Everliving and ever faithful God, who hast given us saints to show us
the path to the right relationship with thee and to stay with us in our
travails: Open our hearts to thy saints that we may join with them in
true dedication to thine only Son our Lord Jesus Christ; through the
same Jesus Christ our Lord, who liveth and reigneth with thee and the
Holy Spirit, one God, for ever and ever. *Amen.*

hymn: all celtic saints

Let us be candles on a stand
and show all the earth the way of thy saints –
Dubricius' light that doth command
the Darkness shrink back and loose its constraints.

Faithful as Brendan let us sail
on oceans unknown, through tempest and shock,
holding thy Way through all travail
with Nonna's tenacious grasp on the rock.

Sitting in quiet Ita's cell,
we listen for thee to give thy command,
even though sacrifice may well
with Cadoc present us into thy hand.

Give us an ounce of Ciaran's grace,
so we might treat others amiably
and create friendships through the race
of humans, as Maedoc showeth for thee.

Show us to care as Brigid did
in love for the hungry, poor, and afraid,
healing the sick who to us bid,
as they did to Beuno for loving aid.

Lead us to learn about thy Word,
as Hildutus did, the better to know
on what great mission for our Lord
with Samson beside us we ought to go.

Ninian's bravery we ask,
to carry us through the trials we face,
looking to Ia in our task –
persistence we need to finish the race.

Let us in all humility
each other serve as Monenna hath shown,
as in Iona's harmony
they did when Columba's hearth warmly shone.

Bring us, oh Lord, to tell thy Deed,
inspired by David's eloquent speech,
also with Samthann do we plead;
true spirituality let us reach.

Show us forgiveness that we may
from Patrick's example all learn to live
firmly united in thy Way,
as thou in thy Cross example dost give.

So let us praise the Lord above
with all of the saints who dwelling below
show us in dedicated love
how we may be saints with spirits aglow.

thanksgiving

We thank thee, Lord, that thou hast given us the example of All Celtic
Saints to guide us to a more perfect dedication in thee.

grace

Almighty and everliving God, by thy Grace let us dedicate ourselves
to thy purpose as have All Celtic Saints.

All Celtic Saints

Joyously

1. Let us be can - dles
3. Sit - ting in qui - et
5. Show us to care as
7. Nin - i - an's bra - ver -

on a stand and
I - ta's cell, we
Brig - id did in
y we ask to

show all the earth the
list - en for thee to
love for the hung - ry,
car - ry us through the

way of thy saints --
give thy com - mand,
poor, and a - fraid,
tri - als we face,

Du - bric - ius' light that
e - ven though sa - cri -
heal - ing the sick who
look - ing to I - a

doth   com -   mand   the
fice   may   well   with
to   us   bid,   as
in   our   task --   per -

Dark -   ness   shrink   back   and
Ca -   doc   pre -   sent   us
they   did   to   Beu -   no
sis -   tence   we   need   to

FINE

loose   its   con -   straints.
in -   to   thy   hand.
for   lov - ing   aid.
fin -   ish   the   race.

222

2. Faith - ful   as   Bren -   dan
4. Give   us   an   ounce   of
6. Lead   us   to   learn   a -
8. Let   us   in   all   hu -

let   us   sail   on
Cia -   ran's   grace,   so
bout   thy   Word,   as
mil -   it -   y   each

o -   ceans   un -   known,   through
we   might   treat   oth -   ers
Hil -   du -   tus   did,   the
oth -   er   serve   as   Mo -

223

tem - pest and shock,
a - mi - ab - ly
bet - ter to know
nen - na hath shown,

hold - ing thy Way through
and cre - ate friend - ships
on what great mis - sion
as in I - o - na's

all tra - vail with
through the race of
for our Lord with
har - mo - ny they

224

penultimate verse D.C. al FINE

Non -	na's	ten -	a -	cious
hu -	mans,	as	Mae -	doc
Sam -	son	be -	side	us
did	when	Co -	lum -	ba's

grasp	on	the	rock.
show -	eth	for	thee.
we	ought	to	go.
hearth	warm -	ly	shown.

9. Bring us, oh Lord, to tell thy Deed,
   inspired by David's eloquent speech,
   also with Samthann do we plead;
   true spirituality let us reach.

10. Show us forgiveness that we may
    from Patrick's example all learn to live
    firmly united in thy Way,
    as thou in thy Cross example dost give.

11. So let us praise the Lord above
    with all of the saints who dwelling below
    show us in dedicated love
    how we may be saints with spirits aglow.

Bibliography and Indices

bibliography

There are a great many books on the saints in general and on the Celtic saints in particular. A few books are recommended here, particularly including those that have been helpful in the compilation of this book.

Bamford, Christopher, and William Parker Marsh. *Celtic Christianity: Ecology and Holiness.* Hudson, New York: Lindisfarne Press, 1987.

Bryce, Derek. *Symbolism of the Celtic Cross.* Felinfach, Dyfed: Llanerch, 1989.

Cahill, Thomas. *How the Irish Saved Civilization: The Untold Story of Ireland's Heroic Role from the Fall of Rome to the Rise of Medieval Europe.* New York: Doubleday, 1995.

Chadwick, Nora. *Celtic Britain.* London: Thames & Hudson, 1963.

Chadwick, Nora. *The Age of the Saints in the Early Celtic Church.* London: Oxford University Press, 1961.

Chadwick, Nora. *The Celts.* London: Pelican, 1971.

Doble, G.H. *Lives of the Welsh Saints,* ed. by D. Simon Evans. Cardiff: University of Wales Press, 1971.

Duncan, Anthony. *The Elements of Celtic Christianity.* Shaftesbury, Dorset: Element, 1992.

Farmer, David Hugh. *The Oxford Dictionary of Saints,* 3rd ed. Oxford: Oxford University Press, 1992.

Ford, Patrick K. (ed). *Celtic Folklore and Christianity.* Santa Barbara, California: McNally & Loftin, 1983.

Henken, Elissa R. *The Welsh Saints: A Study in Patterned Lives.* Cambridge: D.S. Brewer, 1991.

229

Henken, Elissa R. *Traditions of the Welsh Saints*. Cambridge: D.S. Brewer, 1987.

Howlett, D.R. (ed. & trans.). *The Book of Letters of Saint Patrick the Bishop*. Dublin: Four Courts Press, 1994.

Lehane, Brendan. *Early Celtic Christianity*. New York: Barnes & Noble, 1993.

MacDonald, Iain (ed.). *Saint Brendan*. Edinburgh: Floris Books, 1992.

MacDonald, Iain (ed.). *Saint Bride*. Edinburgh: Floris Books, 1992.

MacDonald, Iain (ed.). *Saint Columba*. Edinburgh: Floris Books, 1992.

MacDonald, Iain (ed.). *Saint Patrick*. Edinburgh: Floris Books, 1992.

Mackey, James P. (ed.). *An Introduction to Celtic Christianity*. Edinburgh: T & T Clark, 1989.

McNeill, John T. *The Celtic Churches*. Chicago: University of Chicago Press, 1974.

Mitten, Michael. *The Soul of Celtic Spirituality: In the Lives of its Saints*. Mystic, Connecticut: Twenty-Third Publications. 1996.

Plummer, Charles (ed.). *Lives of Irish Saints*. London: Oxford University Press, 1922.

Pryce, John. *The Ancient British Church: A Historical Essay*. London: Longmans, Green, and Company, 1878.

Raine, Andy, & John T. Skinner (eds.). *Celtic Daily Prayer: A Northumbrian Office*. London: MarshallPickering, 1994.

Sellner, Edward C. *Wisdom of the Celtic Saints*. Notre Dame, Indiana: Ave Maria Press, 1993.

Sharpe, Richard. *Medieval Irish Saints' Lives*. Oxford: Clarendon Press. 1991.

Thomas, Patrick. *Candle in the Darkness: Celtic Spirituality from Wales*. Llandysul, Dyfed: Gomer. 1993.

Touson, Shirley. *The Celtic Year: A Month-by=Month Celebration of Celtic Christian Festivals and Sites*. Shaftesbury, Dorset: Element, 1993.

Van de Weyer, Robert (ed.). *Celtic Fire: The Passionate Religious Vision of Ancient Britain and Ireland*. New York: Doubleday, 1990.

índex of
scripture

The following Scripture verses are quoted in the book. Those in boldface are the lessons that are used in the Holy Scripture portion of the celebrations.

index of saints

index of localities

The following localities (from churches and villages to provinces) in Britain, Ireland, and Brittany are cited by name in the book.